Holmes McDougall
Metric Maths

BOOK 5

J. O'Neill
J. Potts
J. Wood

General Editor: I. D. Watt

Holmes McDougall Ltd

Art-work by F. Vaughan

Printed by Holmes McDougall Ltd., Print Division.

© 1972 Holmes McDougall

SBN 7157 0784-1

Contents   Book 5

INTRODUCTORY NOTE

The whole atmosphere of education has changed in the post-war years, particularly in the last decade. Everywhere, at all stages, there is evident a quickening of interest and a lively urge to try out new ideas and new methods, to provide an education that makes sense to the children of to-day. Teachers are aware, as no-one else, that there is no room for complacency, that we are nearer the beginning than the end of educational development. What can be claimed is that the prospect of sensible and sustained advance is brighter than ever before.

Nowhere is change more evident than in the Primary School. The day of the stereotype in syllabuses and textbooks is quickly going. New subjects have been introduced, old ones refurbished and modernised. Teaching methods are placing greater emphasis on assignments and pupil participation. The stress is on adaptability and the capacity to think creatively. The demand for change has come from the schools themselves. The practising teacher in the classroom is becoming more and more the pacemaker and the initiator of new ideas of what to teach and how to teach.

Of all subjects in the Primary School curriculum, mathematics is the one that is undergoing the greatest change. Up until a few years ago the teaching of the subject was in large part confined to the development of skill in reckoning and the manipulation of unwieldy computations of little relevance and doubtful educational value. Much of the work was of a routine nature, much of it divorced from practical realities, with little understanding of the nature of the underlying concepts This is being changed.

Materials for the study of mathematics—number, quantity and shape— abound in the child's environment and, by means of meaningful experiences, purposefully planned, children are being led progressively to the understanding of basic mathematical concepts. But, as the Memorandum on Primary Education in Scotland points out, there is no suggestion that all the material to be studied can be found directly in the environment or that none of the subjects grouped under Environmental Studies has to be pursued as a separate discipline. In the words of the Memorandum: "Indeed, in the case of mathematics, especially that part of it which is concerned with number, there must be from the earliest stages training in specific skills that will enable the pupils to handle quickly and efficiently the mathematical situations which will arise in the course of their other activities."

In this series of development exercises it is the need for this basic training in specific skills that the authors — all experienced in the day-to-day work of the schools—have had constantly in mind. Drafts of the exercises were tried out in a variety of schools and modified in the light of the reactions of both teachers and pupils. The result is a series of books which, it is confidently expected, will make a distinctive and useful contribution to the teaching of mathematics in primary schools.

Decimals

ABE REMEMBERS—DO YOU?

1

(1) What is the sum of 41·25, 61·73 and 40?
(2) What is the difference between 678·1 and 439·2?
(3) Calculate 79·13 m + 61·25 m + 8·01 m.
(4) Find £26·15 − £15·60.
(5) Subtract 17·34 from 32·36 + 16·85.
(6) What is 16·24 − 17·82 + 21·23?
(7) What change remains out of £20 when bills of £4·24, £8·16 and £3·25 are paid?
(8) A DIY shop has a total of 19·4 m of timber for shelving. Three customers buy lengths amounting to 2·18 m, 10·92 m and 4·72 m respectively and a fourth customer asks for 3 m. Can the DIY shop satisfy the fourth customer? Give a reason for your answer.
(9) Abe has £12·50 with which to pay his bills of £5·25 to the Butcher, £3·65 to the Grocer and £1·20 to the Dairy. How much change is left? Can Abe afford out of his change to pay £2·50 for a bus tour?
(10) A man deposits £20·00 in his bank and thereafter deposits £2·55 weekly over a period of 47 weeks. How much money did he deposit in his account during that period?
(11) A woman arranges to pay a bill of £14·40 at the rate of £2·40 per week. How much does she still owe after 4 weeks? How many more weeks are required to settle the bill?
(12) A petrol pump tank holds 8 000 litres of petrol. From the pump just filled, the following orders were supplied to dealers, 20·5 litres, 8·25 litres, 10·25 litres, 15·75 litres and 35·25 litres. How much petrol still remains in the pump?

DECIMAL MEMORIES

× 10   Move the Digits to the Left

÷ 10   Move the Digits to the Right

× 32·7 means × 30
Then   × 2
Then   × 0·7
Followed by addition.

Find the Answers to:

2

(1) 48·1 × 10	(2) 0·612 × 100	(3) 7·16 × 10
(4) 681 ÷ 10	(5) 71·6 ÷ 100	(6) 82·5 ÷ 10
(7) 62·2 × 30	(8) 85·3 × 50	(9) 7·23 × 60
(10) 62·2 × 0·2	(11) 85·3 × 0·3	(12) 7·23 × 0·4
(13) 62·2 × 35·2	(14) 85·3 × 52·3	(15) 7·23 × 67·4
(16) 72·4 ÷ 20	(17) 24·9 ÷ 30	(18) 64·44 ÷ 40

ABE'S PUZZLERS

3

(1) The cost of a school outing is £0·85 per pupil. What is the total cost to a class of 47 pupils?

(2) What is the total weight of 6 similarly loaded lorries if one of them weighs 3122·5 kg?

(3) Tom scored a total of 354 marks out of a possible 500. Express Tom's score as a percentage of the total possible.

(4) £8 468 is shared equally among 4 people. How much does each get?

(5) Find the cost of a carpet 3·5 m × 2·5 m at £2·44 per m²

(6) On the M6 the speed of a car averaged 68·2 km per hr. What distance was covered by the car in 2·5 hours?

(7) Evaluate: $\dfrac{6·25 \times 3·4}{5}$

(8) Find the value of $(86·25 + 45·93) - (4·25 \times 7·4)$

(9) The average score of a cricket eleven was 21 runs. What was the total of runs scored?

(10) Abe earns £18·75 per week. What are his gross earnings for a year of 52 working weeks? If he pays £2·32 per week for Income Tax how much is this for that year? If he also has deducted £1·98 per week for insurance, and Union dues, what are his net earnings per annum?

DECIMAL DIVISION

Abe has a problem

but Abe remembers

Abe says

Find the answers for:

4

(1) $9 \cdot 2 \times 10$ (2) $2 \cdot 3 \times 10$ (3) $9 \cdot 2 \div 2 \cdot 3$

(4) $11 \cdot 9 \times 10$ (5) $1 \cdot 7 \times 10$ (6) $11 \cdot 9 \div 1 \cdot 7$

(7) $1 \cdot 28 \times 10$ (8) $1 \cdot 6 \times 10$ (9) $1 \cdot 28 \div 1 \cdot 6$

(10) $2 \cdot 09 \div 1 \cdot 9$ (11) $14 \cdot 91 \div 2 \cdot 1$ (12) $7 \cdot 44 \div 2 \cdot 4$

(13) $10 \cdot 85 \div 3 \cdot 5$ (14) $1 \cdot 19 \div 0 \cdot 17$ (15) $0 \cdot 128 \div 0 \cdot 16$

(16) $1 \cdot 491 \div 0 \cdot 21$ (17) $0 \cdot 209 \div 0 \cdot 19$ (18) £$11 \cdot 13 \div 5 \cdot 3$

(19) $14 \cdot 28 \text{ m} \div 6 \cdot 8$ (20) £$164 \cdot 22 \div 2 \cdot 1$ (21) £$135 \cdot 25 \div 2 \cdot 5$

(22) $37 \cdot 5 \text{ kg} \div 7 \cdot 5$ (23) £$108 \cdot 72 \div 3 \cdot 6$ (24) $28 \cdot 80 \text{ m} \div 4 \cdot 80$

(25) $13 \div 3 \cdot 25$

ABE HAS PROBLEMS

5

(1) Find the cost of 1 litre of petrol if $4 \cdot 5$ litres cost £$1 \cdot 44$. What is the cost of $11 \cdot 5$ litres?

(2) Mrs. Brown paid £$1 \cdot 65$ for $1 \cdot 5$ kg of meat. What was the cost of the meat per kilogramme? How much of this meat could be bought for £$2 \cdot 20$?

(3) What is the average daily wage for a man who earns £$32 \cdot 45$ in 5 days?

(4) What is the average speed in km per hour of a car which travels 812 km in 14 hours?

(5) The cost of filling a car with petrol was £$1 \cdot 36\frac{1}{2}$ when petrol was $6\frac{1}{2}$p per litre. How many litres does the tank hold?

(6) Calculate the value of $\dfrac{2 \cdot 35 \times 1 \cdot 3}{1 \cdot 5}$ giving your answer correct to the second decimal place.

(7) The petrol tank in a car holds 50 litres. If the car travels $9 \cdot 6$ km on a litre of petrol, how far can it travel before refuelling?

(8) In $7 \cdot 5$ days a ship travelled 6 300 kilometres. Calculate the average distance covered per day.

(9) Estimate the value of $\dfrac{7 \cdot 25 \times 2 \cdot 4}{2 \cdot 8}$ to the nearest whole number and then calculate the value correct to the first decimal place.

(10) A bucket holds $2 \cdot 7$ litres. How many bucketfuls are needed to fill a water tank measuring 120 cm $\times$ 40 cm $\times$ 36 cm?
(1 litre = 1 000 cm³)

Percentages %

$27\frac{1}{2}\%$ $\dfrac{27\frac{1}{2}}{100} = \dfrac{55}{200}$ $= \dfrac{11}{40}$

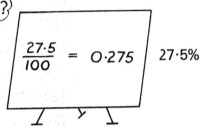

$\dfrac{27\cdot5}{100} = 0\cdot275$ $27\cdot5\%$

6

(1) Write these percentages in fraction form:
(a) 54%   (b) 15%   (c) 30%   (d) 25%   (e) 40%
(f) 76%   (g) $12\frac{1}{2}\%$ (h) $33\frac{1}{3}\%$ (i) $62\frac{1}{2}\%$ (j) $87\frac{1}{2}\%$

(2) Write these percentages in decimal form:
(a) 38%   (b) 49%   (c) 76%   (d) 20%   (e) 5%
(f) 9%   (g) $12\cdot5\%$ (h) $33\cdot3\%$ (i) $7\cdot5\%$ (j) $2\frac{1}{2}\%$

(3) Copy and complete this table:

Percentage	Fraction	Decimal	Percentage	Fraction	Decimal
25%			$12\frac{1}{2}\%$		
10%			$6\frac{1}{4}\%$		
5%			$2\frac{1}{2}\%$		

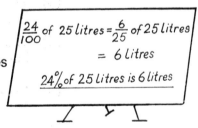

24% of 25 litres = 0·24 x 25 litres
= 6·00 litres
24% of 25 litres is 6 litres

24% of 25 litres

$\dfrac{24}{100}$ of 25 litres = $\dfrac{6}{25}$ of 25 litres
= 6 litres
24% of 25 litres is 6 litres

7

Find the value of:
(1) 20% of 85p   (2) 70% of 90p   (3) 90% of 60p
(4) 25% of £28   (5) 75% of £84   (6) 5% of £400
(7) 8% of £6   (8) 32% of £50   (9) 56% of £300
(10) $2\frac{1}{2}\%$ of 160 litres   (11) $6\cdot5\%$ of £800   (12) $33\frac{1}{3}\%$ of 60 m
(13) 10% of £19·40   (14) 60% of £32·85   (15) 9% of £18
(16) 7% of 600 pupils   (17) 85% of 280 girls   (18) 95% of 320 boys
(19) $12\frac{1}{2}\%$ of £33·60   (20) $2\frac{1}{2}\%$ of £44·80

SERVICE CHARGE AND DISCOUNT

Most hotels add a *service charge* to the bills of their customers.

The service charge replaces 'tipping'.

A *service charge increases* the bill.

Some shops offer a *discount* to customers who pay cash for articles such as furniture.

A *discount decreases* the bill.

Find the total amount paid on a hotel bill for £24 if a service charge of 10% is applied.

Service charge is $\frac{10}{100}$ of £24
$= \frac{1}{10}$ of £24
$= £2\cdot40$
Total amount is £24 + £2·40
or £26·40

Find the cash price paid for a TV set marked at £82 if a 5% discount is given.

Discount is $\frac{5}{100}$ of £82
$= 0\cdot05$ of £82
$= £4\cdot10$
Cash price is £82 − £4·10
or £77·90

8

(1) Increase £40 by 5%
(2) Increase £76 by 10%
(3) Increase £88 by $12\frac{1}{2}$%
(4) Decrease £50 by 6%
(5) Decrease £80 by $2\frac{1}{2}$%
(6) Decrease £48 by 5%
(7) Increase £46·20 by 20%
(8) Decrease £32·80 by 25%
(9) The bill for a dinner party at a hotel was £75. If the service charge was 10%, find the total amount paid.
(10) A man buys £160 of furniture in a store and is allowed a 5% discount on payment by cash. How much does he actually pay?
(11) At Seaway Grand Hotel, the service charge is $12\frac{1}{2}$%. Find the total amount paid for a 'Room and Food' bill of £44·80.
(12) Super Duper Electrics offer colour television sets for sale at £240 on easy terms. Find the amount paid by Mr. Smith who pays cash for a set if the discount given for a cash sale is $2\frac{1}{2}$%.
     How much more would Mr. Smith have paid, if instead of paying cash, he had accepted the easy terms, — deposit £24, together with monthly instalments of £12 over a period of 2 years?
(13) A store allows customers 4% discount if they pay cash within 7 days for goods obtained. Find the actual amount paid by a customer who pays cash for £42 worth of goods.
(14) A man and his wife stayed at the Excelsior Hotel for a week, the terms being £42 per person per week together with a service charge of $12\frac{1}{2}$%. Find the total bill paid.

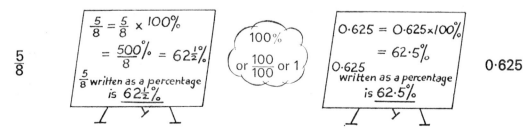

9

9 Express as percentages:

(1) $\frac{1}{4}$ (2) $\frac{1}{5}$ (3) $\frac{3}{10}$ (4) $\frac{2}{5}$ (5) $\frac{9}{20}$

(6) $\frac{14}{25}$ (7) $\frac{47}{50}$ (8) $\frac{1}{8}$ (9) $\frac{7}{8}$ (10) $\frac{2}{3}$

(11) 0·65   (12) 0·46   (13) 0·4   (14) 0·75   (15) 0·345

(16) 0·06   (17) 0·375   (18) 0·02   (19) 0·075   (20) 1·08

PERCENTAGES AND ATTENDANCE

	M	T	W	Th	F	Abs.
John	O					1
David				O O O		3
Charles			O O			2
Paul						—

During a school week, John was absent on Monday afternoon. He thus had 9 out of 10 attendances for the week.

John's percentage attendance was $\frac{9}{10} \times 100\%$ or 90%

How many attendances had David? Charles? Paul?

10

(1) From the register above find the weekly percentage attendance for:
   (a) David   (b) Charles,   (c) Paul

(2) On Monday morning 4 out of 16 boys in the class were absent.   What percentage of the boys were then: (a) Absent,   (b) Present?

(3) On Monday morning 2 out of 20 girls in the above class were absent.   What percentage of the girls were then: (a) Absent,   (b) Present?

(4) From questions (2) and (3), find:
   (a) The number of pupils in the class.
   (b) The number of pupils absent on Monday morning.

   Using the answers to (a) and (b), find the percentage of pupils:
   (c) Absent on Monday morning.
   (d) Present on Monday morning.

(5) During the week there were 360 possible attendances for the class and the total number of absences was 54.
   For the week, find the percentage of pupils: (a) Absent,
   (b) Present.

(6) In another class the total number of possible attendances for the week was 350. The total number of absences was 28.
   Find: (a)   The number of pupils in the class.
   (b)   The percentage of pupils absent during the week.
   (c)   The percentage of pupils present during the week.

Assignment: Ask teacher for the necessary numbers and then find, correct to the nearest whole number, last week's percentage attendance for your class.

Significant Figures

ONE

The following items were reported in the Press:

About 60 000 people attended a Football match at . . . . .
The attendance at the School concert was about 500 . . . . .
There were about 30 people at the party and . . . . .
The car costing about £2 000 . . . . .
The population of City X is about 700 000

The numbers 60 000, 500, 30, 2 000 and 700 000 in the above items have only one significant or meaningful digit, namely, the first digits 6, 5, 3, 2 and 7. These reported numbers which are 'about' or 'approximate' have been *corrected to* or given *correct to* one *significant figure*. Note that since the population of a City such as City X varies from day to day, 700 000 gives a significant indication of the size of the population.

If it had been necessary to state the above items accurately we may have read:

61 237 attended the football match . . . . .
The attendance at the school concert was 512 . . . . .
There were 33 at the party and . . . . .
The car costing £2 112 . . . . .
The population of City X is 732 129 . . . . .

Rule: To write a number 'corrected to' or 'correct to' *one significant figure—examine the second digit and*

(1) If it is 4, 3, 2, 1 or 0 the first digit remains unaltered and all other digits are replaced by zeros.

(2) If it is 5, 6, 7, 8 or 9, the first digit is increased by 1 and all other digits are replaced by zeros.

Note: Zeros are required as place holders.

In the following table the numbers in columns A and B are each 'corrected to' one significant figure and represented by the number in the third column.

A	B	Correct to 1 significant figure
26, 27, 28, 29	31, 32, 33, 34	30
487, 461, 451 450, 499, 472	501, 512, 547 539, 520, 549	500
1 993, 1 500, 1 691 1 873, 1 789, 1 807	2 356, 2 001, 2 499 2 285, 2 393, 2 178	2 000
46 583 724	50 982 568	50 000 000

For each of the following statements, rewrite the 'actual figures' *corrected to one significant figure:*

11

(1) The price of a book is 98p.

(2) The attendance at the concert is 687.

(3) The price of a new car is £2 956.

(4) A new shirt costs £3·25 (325p).

(5) The distance from Glasgow to London is 640 kilometres.

(6) The attendance at the football match was 8 146.

(7) The speed of the plane is 835 kilometres per hour.

(8) The distance round the equator is 40 192 kilometres.

(9) The factory employs 9 754 workers.

(10) There are 955 pupils in the school.

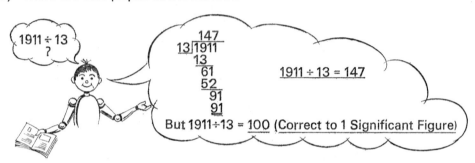

Find the answers to each of the following correct to one significant figure.

12

(1) 40×7

(2) 12×90

(3) $1·7 \times 0·8$

(4) $3·57 \div 3$

(5) $13·99 \div 0·7$

(6) $56p \times 5$

(7) £$1·62 \times 9$

(8) $5·76$ m $\div 4$

(9) $\dfrac{5 \times 4}{6}$

(10) $\dfrac{12 \times 11}{10}$

TWO Significant Figures

The return fare is about £170 . . . . .

The number of teachers in Glasgow is about 7 800, ...

The number of Fire calls for a certain year in Glasgow was about 12 000 . . . . .

Note: In the above statements the numbers **170**, **78**00 and **12** 000 are reported as 'corrected to' *two significant figures.*

Rule: To write a number 'corrected to' two significant figures, *examine the third digit* and:

    (1) If it is 4, 3, 2, 1 or 0 the second digit remains unaltered and all following digits are replaced by *zeros.*

    (2) If it is 5, 6, 7, 8, or 9 the *second digit* is increased by 1 and all following digits are replaced by *zeros.*

In the following table the numbers in columns A and B are each corrected to two significant figures and represented by the number in the third column:

A	B	Correct to 2 significant figures
339, 335, 336, 337	342, 341, 344, 343	340
4 875, 4 869, 4 855 4 890, 4 897, 4 850	4 925, 4 949, 4 912 4 930, 4 901, 4 909	4 900
46 583 724	47 489 999	47 000 000
12·8 12·523	13·4 13·198	13·0 13·000

Write the numbers in each of the following statements correct to *two* significant figures:

13

(1) Glasgow has 1 342 kilometres of public streets.

(2) The distance round the equator is 39 689 kilometres.

(3) The London County Council looks after three-and-a-quarter million people.

(4) Light travels at a speed of 297 600 kilometres per second.

(5) Sound travels at a speed of 1 200 kilometres per hour.

(6) The earth is 148 million kilometres from the sun.

(7) The population of Glasgow has dropped to 927 948.

(8) The human heart beats 4 440 times in one hour.

(9) The cruising speed of 'Concorde' is 2 320 kilometres per hour.

(10) Two-fifths of the world's population, which is 3 070 million, is unable to read and write. Calculate this number and write it correct to two significant figures.

$$\begin{array}{r} 3·6 \\ \times 7 \\ \hline 25·2 \end{array}$$

$3·6 \times 7 = 25·2$
$3·6 \times 7 = 25·0$ correct to 2 significant figures

$$7\overline{)2\ 275} \quad 325$$

$2\ 275 \div 7 = 325$
$2\ 275 \div 7 = 330$ correct to 2 significant figures

Find the answers to each of the following correct to *two* significant figures:

14

(1) 75×43 (2) 184×27 (3) $8\ 523 \div 9$ (4) $6\ 435 \div 13$

(5) $63p \times 52$ (6) $£4·95 \times 12$ (7) $£17·78 \div 14$ (8) $\frac{1}{10}$ of £875

(9) $3·87 \times 0·9$ (10) $2·4 \times 1·7$ (11) $5·64 \times 3·7$ (12) $30·48 \times 1·6$

Powers of Numbers 2^4

$2^4 = 16$

A short way of writing $2 \times 2 \times 2 \times 2$ is 2^4.

The '4' in 2^4 indicates the number of factors 2 being multiplied together. 2^4 is read as to 'two to the power four'.

The value of 2^4 is 16.

Write the following in 'short form' and find the value of each:

15

(1) 2×2 (2) $2 \times 2 \times 2$ (3) $2 \times 2 \times 2 \times 2$ (4) $2 \times 2 \times 2 \times 2 \times 2$
(5) 3×3 (6) $3 \times 3 \times 3$ (7) $3 \times 3 \times 3 \times 3$ (8) $3 \times 3 \times 3 \times 3 \times 3$
(9) 4×4 (10) $4 \times 4 \times 4$ (11) $4 \times 4 \times 4 \times 4$ (12) $4 \times 4 \times 4 \times 4 \times 4$
(13) 5×5 (14) $5 \times 5 \times 5$ (15) 6×6 (16) $6 \times 6 \times 6$
(17) 7×7 (18) $7 \times 7 \times 7$ (19) 8×8 (20) $8 \times 8 \times 8$
(21) 9×9 (22) $9 \times 9 \times 9$ (23) 10×10 (24) $10 \times 10 \times 10$

$$3^4 = 3 \times 3 \times 3 \times 3$$
$$= 9 \times 9$$
$$= 81$$

$$3 \times 5^2 = 3 \times 5 \times 5$$
$$= 3 \times 25$$
$$= 75$$

Find the value of:

16

(1) 2^4 (2) 4^2 (3) 2^6 (4) 6^2 (5) 3^5 (6) 5^3
(7) 9^3 (8) 8^2 (9) 10^2 (10) 10^4 (11) 2×3^4 (12) 2×3^3
(13) 2×3^2 (14) 3×2^2 (15) 3×2^3 (16) 3×2^4 (17) 3×2^5 (18) 5×3^2
(19) 4×3^2 (20) 3×3^2 (21) 3×4^3 (22) 2×4^3 (23) 3×4^2 (24) 4×4^2
(25) 6×5^2 (26) 5×6^2 (27) 2×9^2 (28) 9×2^2 (29) 9×10^3 (30) 5×10^4

Copy and complete:

17

(1) $12 = 3 \times 4 = 3 \times 2^2$
$16 = 4 \times 4 = 4 \times 2^2$
$20 = 5 \times \quad = $
$24 = 6 \times \quad = $
$28 = 7 \times \quad = $
$32 = \quad = $
$36 = \quad = $
$40 = \quad = $

(2) $18 = 2 \times 9 = 2 \times 3^2$
$27 = 3 \times \quad = $
$36 = 4 \times \quad = $
$45 = 5 \times \quad = $
$54 = \quad = $
$63 = \quad = $
$72 = \quad = $
$81 = \quad = $
$90 = \quad = $

18

(1) Write as powers of 2 only:
(a) 4 (b) 8 (c) 16 (d) 32 (e) 64

(2) Write as powers of 3 only:
(a) 9 (b) 27 (c) 81 (d) 243 (e) 729

14

Proportion

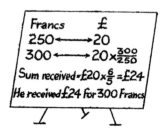

A French tourist received £20 for 250 francs. How much will he receive in exchange for 300 francs?

19

(1) 8 cakes cost 28p. What will 12 similar cakes cost?
(2) If 4 plugs cost 72p, find the cost of 5 similar plugs.
(3) A boy takes 5 minutes to walk 400 metres. How far can he walk in 3 minutes at the same rate?
(4) If 9 litres of petrol are needed for a car to travel 78 km, how far can the car travel on 15 litres of petrol?
(5) If 300 eggs cost £5·40, how much should 250 of these eggs cost?

(6)
A group of 5 musicians take 260 seconds to play a piece of music. How long should a group of 3 players take to play the same piece?

(7) Find the cost of 9 machines if 21 similar machines cost £245.
(8) A man is paid the same amount each week. He earns £264 in 11 weeks. How long will it take him to earn £336?

INDIRECT PROPORTION

A girl gets a present of a book-token and finds that the number of books she can get at various prices are as follows:

Price of Book	Number of books
10p	20
20p	10
25p	8
40p	5
50p	4
£1	2
?	1

What was the value of the book-token?
Check that each line in the above table is correct.

Note: As the price is doubled, the number of books is halved.
As the number of books is quadrupled, the price per book is quartered.
Quantities which bear such relationships to each other are said to be in *indirect proportion.*

A polar expedition has enough food to last 16 men for 18 weeks. How long will the same supply last 24 men?

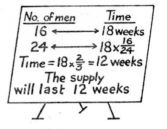

20

(1) 12 men take 5 days to paint a building. How long will it take 1 man to paint a similar building if he works at the same rate?

(2) A man can erect a car from a car-building kit in 30 hours. How long will it take 3 men to erect a similar car from a similar kit?

(3) A farmer has enough oats to feed 9 horses for 10 days. How long will the same supply of oats feed 6 horses?

(4) With record-tokens a girl can buy 8 records at 40p each. At what price per record could she buy 10 records with the same tokens?

(5) A boy walks direct from home to school at a speed of 6 km/hour in 14 minutes. How long will the same journey take him at a speed of 7 km/hour?

(6) If a packet of sweets is divided among 20 children, they each get 6 sweets. How many sweets will each get if the packet is divided among 30 children?

(7) A cyclist can complete a lap of a track in 40 seconds travelling at 42 km/hour. At what speed must he cycle to complete a lap in 35 seconds?

(8) If 24 men can build a jetty in 15 months, how many men will build the jetty in 12 months?

(9) A Riding School has enough fodder to feed 12 ponies for 20 days. If the number of ponies is increased to 15, how long will the fodder last?

(10) If 15 men can load a ship in 10 days, how many extra men must be employed to load the ship in 6 days?

ABE'S MIXTURES

21

(1) 8 metres of cloth costs £18. What is the cost of 10 metres of this cloth?

(2) If 24 bars of chocolate cost £1·92, find the cost of 9 of the bars.

(3) A camp leader has enough crisps to give each of 40 children 9 packets. If only 36 children want crisps, how many packets can each get?

(4) £8 buys 104 French francs. How many francs will £14 buy?

(5) If it takes 45 minutes to bake 8 Honeycakes in an oven, how long will it take to bake 6 Honeycakes in the oven?

(6) In 8 weeks a man earns £232·80. How much should he earn in 15 weeks?

(7) A car travelling at 60 km/hour takes 8 hours to complete a journey. At what speed must another car travel to complete the same journey in 12 hours?

(8) A factory employs 42 men to assemble 720 machines in a week. How many extra men must be employed to assemble 840 machines in a week?

Subsets

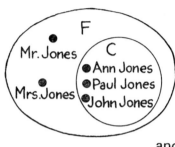

This ring picture illustrates the two sets:

F = {Mr. Jones, Mrs. Jones, Ann Jones, Paul Jones, John Jones }

and C = {Ann Jones, Paul Jones, John Jones }

Every member of set C is also a member of set F

    We say   C is a **subset** of F

    We write C   ⊂   F

In this example, F could be described as the set of the Jones family and C could be described as the set of the Jones children.

In this ring picture,

    V = {cabbage, lettuce, turnip, apple, lemon, carrot, orange, onion }

and F = {apple, lemon, orange }

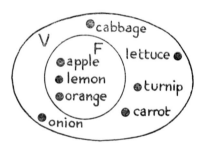

        F ⊂ V   That is, F is a subset of V.

Since the set V has a very large number of subsets, we shall consider the set F which has 8 subsets:

(1) {apple }   (2) {lemon }

(3) {orange }   (4) {apple, lemon }

(5) {apple, orange }   (6) {lemon, orange }

(7) {apple, lemon, orange } (8) {   }

We may write,   {orange, lemon } ⊂ F ⊂ V.

Note: (a) Subsets are sets included within sets.

      (b) The empty set is a subset of all sets.

      (c) Each set is a subset of itself.

      (d) The sign ⊄ means *is not a subset of.*

$$T = \{3, 6, 9, 12, 15\}$$
$$S = \{6, 12\}$$
$$S \subset T$$

$$V = \{a, e, i, o, u\}$$
$$W = \{w, o, r, d\}$$
$$W \not\subset V$$

22

(1) Look at Abe's blackboards then copy and complete these sentences:
  (a) The members of set S are also members of set............
  (b) Set S is a .... of set T.
  (c) S ⊂ T means that set S is a .... of set T.
  (d) S ... T means that set S is a subset of set T.
  (e) W ⊄ V means that set W is not a .... of set V.
  (f) W ...V means that set W is not a subset of set V.

(2) List 3 subsets of each of the following sets:
  (a) {4, 8, 12, 16, 20 }   (b) {cat, dog, canary, rabbit}
  (c) The set of pupils in your class   (d) The set of teachers in your school.

(3) List the four subsets of {4, 9 }

(4) List the two subsets of {5 }

(5) List the eight subsets of {red, white, blue}

(6) List the eight subsets of {6, 12, 18}

(7) Using the subsets given, list sets A, B and C each of which has three members:
  (a) {2, 4 } ⊂ A,   {2, 6 } ⊂ A,   {4 } ⊂ A
  (b) {1 } ⊂ B,   { } ⊂ B,   {5, 9 } ⊂ B
  (c) {□, O } ⊂ C,   {O, △ } ⊂ C,   {△, □ } ⊂ C

(8) Using the subsets given, list sets D, E and F each of which has four members:
  (a) {1, 4 } ⊂ D,   {1, 9 } ⊂ D,   {4, 16 } ⊂ D
  (b) {6, 7 } ⊂ E,   {7 } ⊂ E,   { } ⊂ E,   {2, 5 } ⊂ E
  (c) {12 } ⊂ F,   {3, 12 } ⊂ F,   {7 } ⊂ F,   {12, 18 } ⊂ F

(9) From the sets, G = {cup, saucer },   H = {cat, tiger, lion, leopard }
            I = {2, 4, 6, 8, 10 },   J = {plate, saucer, cup, jug }
            K = {4, 8 },   and   L = {5, 10, 15, 20 }

  replace each △ with ⊂ or ⊄ to make each of the following sentences true:
  (a) {tiger } △ H   (b) {4, 6 } △ I   (c) {25 } △ L
  (d) G △ J,   (e) { } △ K   (f) K △ I
  (g) J △ G,   (h) {4, 8 } △ K,   (i) K △ L

(10) List the sixteen subsets of {a, b, c, d }.

VENN DIAGRAMS

The pictures or diagrams shown below represent sets. These pictures are called *Venn Diagrams.*

The members of a set are represented in a Venn Diagram by points inside the boundary of the shape, thus:

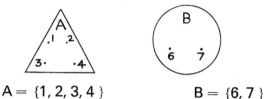 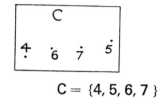

A = {1, 2, 3, 4}   B = {6, 7}   C = {4, 5, 6, 7}

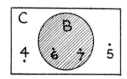

This Venn Diagram shows the relation between the sets B and C where the shaded area represents {6, 7}.

Note: B ⊂ C

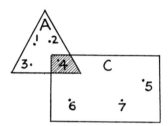

This Venn Diagram shows the relation between the sets A and C where the shaded area represents {4}

Note: {4} ⊂ A and {4} ⊂ C

23

(1)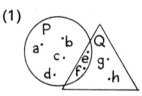

List sets P and Q

(2)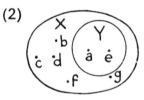

List sets X and Y

(3)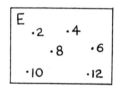

List sets E and T

(4) Copy the following diagrams and insert the members of each set into the correct region:

(a)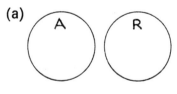

(b)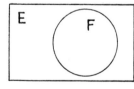

(c)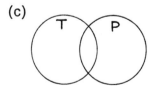

A = {1, 2, 3, 4, }
R = {p, q, r}

E = {1, 2, 3, 4, 5, 6, }
F = {3, 6}

T = {3, 6, 9, 12}
P = {4, 8, 12, 16}

(5) Draw Venn Diagrams to represent each of the following:
  (a) C = {4, 5, 6, 7}, D = {6, 7, 8, 9, 10} (b) G = {a, b, c, d, e, f}, H = {a, e}
  (c) K = {1, 2, 3, 4}, L = {r, s, t}   (d) M, the set of all even numbers,
                                      N, the set of all multiples of 5.

Venn Diagrams are often drawn thus:

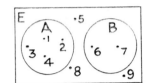 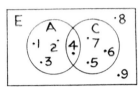 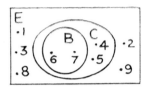

The enclosing rectangle, named E, represents the *Universal Set*. The sets represented within the rectangle are subsets of E.

From the Venn Diagrams, E = {1, 2, 3, 4, 5, 6, 7, 8, 9 },
A = {1, 2, 3, 4 }, B = {6, 7 } and C = {4, 5, 6, 7 }

24

(1)

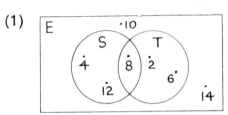

List sets S, T and E

(2)

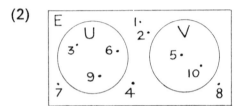

List sets U, V and E

(3)

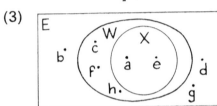

Lists set W, X and E

(4)

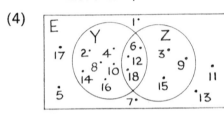

List sets Y, Z and E

(5) Copy the following diagrams and insert the members of set E into the correct regions:

(a)

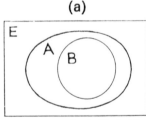

E = {1, 2, 3, 4, 5, 6, 7, 8 }
A = {6, 7, 8, }
B = {7 }

(b)

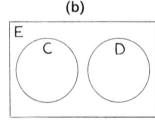

E = {2, 4, 6, 8, 10, 12 }
C = {6, 12 }
D = {4, 10 }

(c)

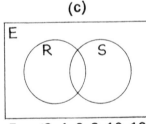

E = {2, 4, 6, 8, 10, 12, 14, 16, 18 }
R = {4, 8, 12, 16 }
S = {6, 8, 10, 12 }

(6) Draw Venn Diagrams to illustrate each of the following:
  (a) E = {1, 2, 3, 4, 5 }, D = {2, 3, 4 }, F = {5 }
  (b) E = {1, 3, 5, 7, 9 }, G = {1, 5, 9 }, H = {7, 9 }
  (c) E = {1, 2, 3, 4, 5, 6, 7, 8 }, K = {2, 4, 6, 8 }, L = {4, 8 }
  (d) E = {a, b, c, d, e, f, g }, M = {a, c, e }, N = {c, d, e }
  (e) E = {a, b, c, d, e, f, g }, P = {c, d, e, f }, Q = {e }
  (f) E = {1, 2, 3, 4, 5, 6, 7, 8, 9, 10 }, A = {3, 4, 5, 6 }, B = {8, 9, 10 }
  (g) E is the set of the first twelve letters in the alphabet. F is the set of letters in the word 'face'. B is the set of letters in the word 'back'.

The Basic Operations

+, ×, −, ÷

Multiplication is a Form of Addition

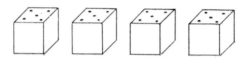

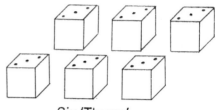

Four 'Fives'
$5 + 5 + 5 + 5 = \mathbf{4 \times 5}$

Six 'Threes'
$3 + 3 + 3 + 3 + 3 + 3 = \mathbf{6 \times 3}$

Note: In mathematics, numbers are often *replaced by symbols* such as □, △, a, b, c, n, p, x, y, z . . . . .

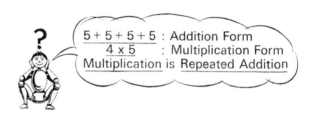

$5 + 5 + 5 + 5$: Addition Form
$\underline{4 \times 5}$: Multiplication Form
Multiplication is Repeated Addition

25 Write in Multiplication Form:
(1) $6 + 6 + 6$
(2) $9 + 9 + 9 + 9$
(3) $7 + 7 + 7 + 7 + 7$
(4) $2 + 2$
(5) $8 + 8 + 8 + 8 + 8 + 8$
(6) $5 + 5 + 5 + 5 + 5$
(7) $3 + 3 + 3 + 3$
(8) $4 + 4 + 4$
(9) $n + n + n$
(10) $b + b + b + b + b$
(11) $y + y$
(12) $x + x + x + x$
(13) $3 + 3 + 3 + \ldots \ldots$ to 8 terms
(14) $6 + 6 + 6 + \ldots \ldots$ to 9 terms
(15) $n + n + n + \ldots \ldots$ to 10 terms
(16) $a + a + a + \ldots \ldots$ to 12 terms
(17) $10 + 10 + 10 + \ldots \ldots$ to n terms
(18) $12 + 12 + 12 + \ldots \ldots$ to a terms
(19) $b + b + b + \ldots \ldots$ to a terms
(20) $a + a + a + \ldots \ldots$ to b terms

$4 \times 1 = \underline{1 + 1 + 1 + 1}$
$3 \times d = \underline{d + d + d}$
$k \times 7 = 7 + 7 + 7 + \cdots \text{to}$
k terms

26 Write out in Addition Form:
(1) 3×4
(2) 2×3
(3) 4×7
(4) 3×5
(5) 4×6
(6) 5×1
(7) 6×2
(8) 1×10
(9) 3×0
(10) 10×8
(11) $3 \times △$
(12) $2 \times □$
(13) $5 \times a$
(14) $4 \times b$
(15) $6 \times c$
(16) $n \times 7$
(17) $p \times 5$
(18) $x \times 9$
(19) $y \times 2$
(20) $z \times 8$

The Commutative Laws

27

(1) Find the value of:
(a) $6+3$ (b) $3+6$ (c) $17+7$ (d) $7+17$ (e) $72+8$ (f) $8+72$
(g) $6-3$ (h) $3-6$ (i) 6×3 (j) 3×6 (k) 10×7 (l) 7×10
(m) 4×5 (n) 5×4 (o) $6\div3$ or $\frac{6}{3}$ (p) $3\div6$ or $\frac{3}{6}$

(2) (a) Is the value of $6+3$ equal to the value of $3+6$?
(b) Is the value of $17+7$ equal to the value of $7+17$?
(c) Is the value of $72+8$ equal to the value of $8+72$?
(d) When *adding* two numbers together, is *the order of addition* important?

> **The Commutative Law of Addition**
> If a and b are any two numbers, then $a+b=b+a$

(3) (a) Is the value of $6-3$ equal to the value of $3-6$?
(b) When *subtracting* one number from another, is *the order of subtraction* important?

> Subtraction is *not* commutative.

(4) (a) Is the value of 6×3 equal to the value of 3×6?
(b) Is the value of 10×7 equal to the value of 7×10?
(c) Is the value of 4×5 equal to the value of 5×4?
(d) When *multiplying* one number by another, is *the order of multiplication* important?

> **The Commutative Law of Multiplication**
> If a and b are any two numbers, then $a\times b=b\times a$

(5) (a) Is the value of $6\div3$ equal to the value of $3\div6$?
(b) Is the value of $\frac{6}{3}$ equal to the value of $\frac{3}{6}$?
(c) When *dividing* one number by another, is *the order of division* important?

> Division is *not* commutative.

(6) (a) Is the result of turning left and then walking 4 paces forward the same as the result of walking 4 paces forward and then turning left?
(b) Is 'turn left' and then '4 paces forward' commutative?

(7) Which of the following are commutative?
(a) 'Right turn' and then 'left turn'.
(b) '4 steps forward' and then '5 steps forward'.
(c) 'Put on your coat' and then 'button up your coat'.
(d) $12+4$. (e) $12-4$. (f) 12×4, (g) $12\div4$.
(h) 'Put on your shoes' and then 'put on your socks'.

(8) 'The Commutative Laws, $a+b=b+a$ and $a\times b=b\times a$, have no exceptions.'
Check that this statement is true by replacing a and b with your own choice of numbers.

Using a Commutative Law

In Mathematics a *shorter form* for $4 \times x$ is $4x$ and a *shorter form* for $a \times b$ is ab.
Thus for $4 \times y$ we may write $4y$

$x \times y$ we may write xy

yx we may write xy (Commutative Law of Multiplication)

$x \times 4$ we may write $4x$ $(x \times 4 = 4 \times x)$

Note: When writing products it is usual to write any numerical factor first followed by any literal or letter factors in alphabetical order.

Thus: $x \times 100$ is written $100x$

$c \times b \times a \times 5$ is written $5abc$.

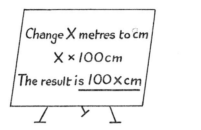

10 millimetres = 1 cm.

1000 millimetres = 1 metre

28

(1) Write in shorter form:

(a) $5 \times a$ (b) $7 \times b$ (c) $8 \times c$ (d) $6 \times d$ (e) $p \times 3$ (f) $q \times 2$

(g) $r \times 9$ (h) $s \times 4$ (i) $x + x$ (j) $y + y + y$ (k) $a \times b$ (l) $b \times a$

(2) Change the given quantities to the units stated:

(a) £m to pence   (b) n cm to millimetres   (c) h hours to minutes

(d) k kg to grammes   (e) w weeks to days   (f) £p to 'fifties'

(g) d days to hours   (h) k litres to millilitres   (i) 4m metres to centimetres

SPEED TEST

Complete column (a) first, then column (b), then column (c) and finally column (d). Write answers only. Practice until you can 'beat the clock' in 7 minutes.

29

	(a)	(b)	(c)	(d)
(1)	$3 + 5$	$13 + 5$	$(5 + 7) + 3$	$(2 \times 8) + 4$
(2)	$6 + 7$	$4 + 15$	$(10 + 7) - 6$	$8 + (7 \times 2)$
(3)	$4 + 6$	$13 + 8$	$23 - (15 - 7)$	$(15 \div 3) + 18$
(4)	$8 - 4$	$23 - 4$	$7 + (4 \times 8)$	$(5 \times 7) - 4$
(5)	$11 - 5$	$26 - 9$	$(3 \times 7) - 12$	$31 - (24 \div 8)$
(6)	$16 - 7$	$42 - 8$	$8 + (9 + 3)$	$42 - (30 \div 5)$
(7)	3×5	7×9	$17 \div 4$	$(2 \times 5) \times 6$
(8)	6×4	8×8	$19 \div 5$	$3 \times (4 \times 2)$
(9)	5×6	7×8	$24 \div 7$	$10 \times (3 \times 2)$
(10)	$18 \div 2$	$42 \div 6$	$32 \div 5$	$(45 \div 9) \times 8$
(11)	$28 \div 7$	$72 \div 8$	$75 \div 9$	$27 \div (21 \div 7)$
(12)	$48 \div 6$	$45 \div 9$	$52 \div 7$	$(10 \times 4) \div 5$

The Associative Laws

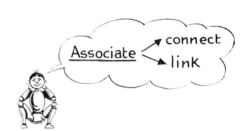

Associate → connect
→ link

30

(1) Find the value of:

(a) $8 + (5 + 2)$ (b) $(8 + 5) + 2$ (c) $9 + (7 + 6)$ (d) $(9 + 7) + 6$
(e) $7 + (6 + 4)$ (f) $(7 + 6) + 4$ (g) $8 - (5 - 2)$ (h) $(8 - 5) - 2$
(i) $8 \times (5 \times 2)$ (j) $(8 \times 5) \times 2$ (k) $2 \times (10 \times 3)$ (l) $(2 \times 10) \times 3$
(m) $4 \times (2 \times 3)$ (n) $(4 \times 2) \times 3$ (o) $12 \div (6 \div 2)$ (p) $(12 \div 6) \div 2$

(2) (a) Is the value of $8 + (5 + 2)$ equal to the value of $(8 + 5) + 2$?
    (b) Is the value of $9 + (7 + 6)$ equal to the value of $(9 + 7) + 6$?
    (c) Replace a with 7, b with 6 and c with 4 and check the following law:

The Associative Law of Addition
If a, b and c are any three numbers, then $a + (b + c) = (a + b) + c$

(3) Is the value of $8 - (5 - 2)$ equal to the value of $(8 - 5) - 2$?

Subtraction is *not* associative.

(4) (a) Is the value of $8 \times (5 \times 2)$ equal to the value of $(8 \times 5) \times 2$?
    (b) Is the value of $2 \times (10 \times 3)$ equal to the value of $(2 \times 10) \times 3$?
    (c) Replace a with 4, b with 2 and c with 3 and check:

The Associative Law of Multiplication
If a, b and c are any three numbers, then $a(bc) = (ab)c$

(5) Is the value of $12 \div (6 \div 2)$ equal to the value of $(12 \div 6) \div 2$?

Division is *not* associative.

(6) If $\triangle$, $\square$ and $\lozenge$ are replacements for natural numbers, which of the following operations are associative?
    (a) $\triangle + (\square + \lozenge)$ (b) $(\triangle - \square) - \lozenge$
    (c) $(\triangle \times \square) \times \lozenge$ (d) $\triangle \div (\square \div \lozenge)$

(7) Find the answers to the following in the easiest possible way:
(a) $16 + 53 + 7$ (b) $2 \times 5 \times 9$ (c) $71 + 9 + 5$
(d) $14 \times 5 \times 2$ (e) $91 + 9 + 76$ (f) $38 \times 2 \times 5$
(g) $83 + (17 + 41)$ (h) $12 + 36 + 88$ (i) $5 \times (20 \times 33)$
(j) $65 + 46 + 35$ (k) $2 \times 84 \times 5$ (l) $4 \times 17 \times 25$

(8) 'The Associative Laws for Addition and Multiplication, $a + (b + c) = (a + b) + c$ and $a(bc) = (ab)c$, have no exceptions'.
Check that this statement is true by replacing a, b and c with your own choice of numbers.

Progress Checks

PROGRESS CHECK 1

(1) On three consecutive days, a shopkeeper deposits £27·55, £59·40 and £32·85 in the bank. Find the total deposited.

(2) A sack contains 66 kg of flour. How many packets, each containing 1·5 kg, can be filled from the sack?

(3) Write 7·5% in decimal form.

(4) Express $\frac{7}{20}$ as a percentage.

(5) Write correct to two significant figures:
$\qquad$ (a) 3 760 $\qquad$ (b) 195 700 $\qquad$ (c) 10·95

(6) Find 0·25 × £9·12. Give your answer correct to two significant figures.

(7) Find the value of $2^3 \times 2^4$.

(8) An American can get £20 in exchange for 55 dollars. What should he get in exchange for 88 dollars?

(9) Draw a Venn Diagram to illustrate the following sets:
$E = \{1, 2, 3, 4, 5, 6, 7, 8\}$, $X = \{1, 2, 4, 8\}$ and $Y = \{1, 4\}$.

(10) Write in shorter form: b × 4 × c.

PROGRESS CHECK 2

(1) A man had £86·24 in his account at the bank. On withdrawing £18·75, how much had he left in his account?

(2) An apprentice gets £7·45 per week. Find his total pay for a year.

(3) Find 15% of £15·00.

(4) Increase £84 by 10%.

(5) Find $\frac{3}{4}$ of 584. Give your answer correct to two significant figures.

(6) Find the value of $2^3 \times 3^2$.

(7) During a certain week a shop gives customers 5% discount on all goods bought. Find the actual amount paid that week for a colour television set which is normally sold at £268.

(8) Express y years in months.

(9) List eight subsets of {red, amber, green}.

(10) Draw a Venn Diagram to illustrate the following sets:
$E = \{1, 2, 3, 4, 5, 6, 7, 8\}$, $A = \{3, 6\}$ and $B = \{1, 4\}$.

PROGRESS CHECK 3

(1) Mother's total electric bill for a year is £54·35. If the first three bills were £15·27, £12·95 and £10·76, find the amount of the remaining bill.

(2) How many bottles, each containing 0·7 litres, can be filled from a 200 litre barrel of spirit ?

(3) Express as a percentage 0·325.

(4) Find the value of $12\frac{1}{2}\%$ of £46·80.

(5) Find the answer to 25·5 × 3·4, correct to two significant figures.

(6) Find the value of $5^2 \times 3^3$. Give your answer correct to two significant figures.

(7) Write in full the number represented by $4·75 \times 10^5$.

(8) List the set S with 4 members given that:
$\{1, 9\} \subset S$, $\{4, 9\} \subset S$ and $\{16\} \subset S$.

(9) During a school year Alan had 384 attendances out of a possible 400 attendances. Find Alan's percentage attendance for the year.

(10) A racing driver can complete one lap of a race in 2 minutes and 5 seconds if he travels at 140 km/hour. Will it take him more time or less time if he travels at 175 km/hour? How long will it take him to complete a lap at 175 km/hour?

NOTE
This Venn Diagram illustrates the relation between three important sets of numbers:

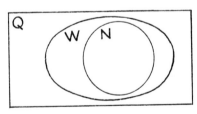

W,   the set of all whole numbers $W = \{0, 1, 2, 3, 4, \ldots\ldots\ldots\}$
N,   the set of all natural numbers $N = \{1, 2, 3, 4, \ldots\ldots\}$
Q,   the set of all rational numbers, that is the set of all whole numbers and fractions.

Using the Commutative and Associative Laws

WHOLE NUMBERS

Addition

$18 + 76 + 82 = 18 + 82 + 76$ *Commutative Law*
$ = (18 + 82) + 76$ *Associative Law*
$ = 100 + 76$

The result is 176

Multiplication

$5 \times 37 \times 20 = 5 \times 20 \times 37$
$ = (5 \times 20) \times 37$
$ = 100 \times 37$

The result is 3 700

$18 + 76 + 82 = (18 + 82) + 76$
The result is 176
$5 \times 37 \times 20 = (5 \times 20) \times 37$
The result is 3 700

31 Using the method on Abe's board, find the answers to:

(1) $9 + 7 + 51$ (2) $44 + 9 + 6$ (3) $98 + 43 + 2$ (4) $87 + 56 + 13$
(5) $5 \times 9 \times 2$ (6) $2 \times 13 \times 5$ (7) $4 \times 8 \times 5$ (8) $20 \times 12 \times 5$
(9) $14 + 18 + 26$ (10) $25 \times 8 \times 4$ (11) $5 \times 9 \times 20$ (12) $35 + 47 + 15$
(13) $10 \times 15 \times 10$ (14) $63 + 78 + 37$ (15) $58 + 29 + 42$ (16) $25 \times 26 \times 4$
(17) $38 + 95 + 62$ (18) $4 \times 64 \times 25$ (19) $89 + 66 + 11$ (20) $5 \times 93 \times 20$

Addition

$3 + x + 4 = 3 + 4 + x$
$ = (3 + 4) + x$
$ = 7 + x$

Commutative Law
Associative Law

The result is $7 + x$

Multiplication

$3 \times x \times 4 = 3 \times 4 \times x$
$ = (3 \times 4) \times x$
$ = 12 \times x$

The result is 12x

$3 + X + 4 = 7 + X$
$3 \times X \times 4 = 12 X$

32 Write in shorter form:

(1) $a + 5 + 9$ (2) $4 \times p \times q$ (3) $8 \times r \times s$ (4) $2 \times 3 \times b$
(5) $3 + 9 + c$ (6) $6 \times 3 \times k$ (7) $6 + x + 3$ (8) $1 \times 7 \times m$
(9) $4 \times n \times 2$ (10) $p \times 3 \times 5$ (11) $q \times 4 \times 6$ (12) $r \times 5 \times s$
(13) $u \times v \times 2$ (14) $6 + y + 7$ (15) $4b \times c$ (16) $d \times 3e$
(17) $5p \times q \times 2$ (18) $4 + c + 1$ (19) $2 \times a \times 3 \times b$ (20) $6x \times 4z$

Note: The use, where possible, of the Commutative and the Associative Laws simplifies calculations in addition and multiplication.

Example:　Add　37
66
65
44
83
———
295

In Units
$(7 + 3) + (6 + 4) + 5 = 25$
In Tens
$(2 + 8) + (4 + 6) + (6 + 3)$
$= 29$

CALCULATIONS WITH WHOLE NUMBERS

33

(1) Add:

(a)		(b)		(c)		(d)		(e)	
	74		48		312		1 327		33 166
	25		215		283		2 741		42 857
	32		306		90		7 685		95 684
	43		47		865		208		7 029

(2) Find the answers for:
   (a) 29 + 207 + 54 + 731 　　(b) 256 + 332 + 108 + 25 + 234
   (c) 1 234 + 6 579 + 8 096 　　(d) 7 262 + 4 865 + 5 107 + 3 983
   (e) 36 274 + 62 105 + 55 307 + 49 486 + 78 790 + 1 023

(3) Subtraction:

(a)		(b)		(c)		(d)		(e)	
	94		203		324		7 826		15 873
	−78		−121		−125		−3 579		−6 783

(4) Find the answers for:
   (a) 546 − 358 　　(b) 921 − 322 　　(c) 40 314 − 16 251
   (d) 5 312 − 2 630 　　(e) 52 640 − 8 953 　　(f) 112 834 − 17 460
   (g) 347 520 − 258 640

(5) Find the products for:
   (a) 3 × 27 　　(b) 325 × 6 　　(c) 109 × 7 　　(d) 8 × 478
   (e) 656 × 9 　　(f) 42 × 40 　　(g) 31 × 51 　　(h) 62 × 43
   (i) 19 × 19 　　(j) 246 × 72 　　(k) 34 × 319 　　(l) 587 × 68

(6) Find the answers for:
   (a) 108 ÷ 2 　　(b) 312 ÷ 4 　　(c) 504 ÷ 6 　　(d) 738 ÷ 9
   (e) 3 425 ÷ 5 　　(f) 3 794 ÷ 7 　　(g) 759 ÷ 33 　　(h) 3 240 ÷ 81
   (i) 3 510 ÷ 54 　　(j) 5 796 ÷ 69 　　(k) 18 942 ÷ 82 　　(l) 34 875 ÷ 75

ABE's MIXTURES

34

(1) Find □ if 547 + □ = 1 324.
(2) A box of chalk contains 144 sticks. How many sticks are there in 7 full boxes?
(3) A car uses 9 litres of petrol to travel 117 km. How far does the car travel on 1 litre of petrol?
(4) In the General Election, 1970, the result at St. Marylebone was declared as shown:
   (a) How many people voted in St. Marylebone?
   (b) Study the figures and find the meaning of 'majority'.

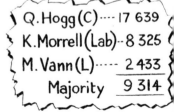

Q. Hogg (C) ···· 17 639
K. Morrell (Lab) ·· 8 325
M. Vann (L) ····· 2 433
Majority　9 314

(5) Find □ if (38 × 28) − 96 = □.

(6) Find n if n = 1 022 + (4 914 ÷ 63)

(7) Add the smallest of the following numbers to the largest:

7 536, 6 753, 3 675, 5 367

(8) 183 500 copies of a Daily Newspaper are printed each day. How many copies of this newspaper are printed in one week?

(9) 630 people are going on an outing in 44 seater buses:
   (a) What is the least number of buses needed to ensure everyone has a seat?
   (b) How many empty seats will there be?

(10) Scoring in Archery is as follows:

Gold 9 points; Red 7 points; Blue 5 points;

Black 3 points; White 1 point; Miss 0 points.

In a competition:
   (a) Derek scored 1 Gold, 3 Red, 5 Blue, 10 Black, 13 White and 4 Misses. Find the total number of points Derek scored.
   (b) Stewart scored 1 Gold, 2 Red, 6 Blue, 15 Black, 7 White and 5 Misses. Find the total number of points Stewart scored.
   (c) Ian scored 2 Gold, 3 Red, 14 Blue, 8 Black, 5 White and 4 Misses. Find out the total number of points Ian scored.
   (d) Place the three competitors in order of merit.

(11) From question (10) what was the maximum possible score in the competition?

The Distributive Law

35   (1)   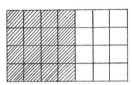

Find □:

(a)   (i)   Total number of squares = 4 × 7 = □
     (ii)   Total number of shaded squares = 4 × 4 = □
    (iii)   Total number of white squares = 4 × 3 = □
     Note: 4 + 3 = 7
               4 × 7 = 4 × (4 + 3)
       So 4 × 7 = (4 × 4) + (4 × 3)

(b)   (i)   Total number of squares = 7 × 4 = □
     (ii)   Total number of dotted squares = 7 × 3 = □
    (iii)   Total number of white squares = 7 × 1 = □
     Note: 3 + 1 = 4
               7 × 4 = 7 × (3 + 1)
       So 7 × 4 = (7 × 3) + (7 × 1)

(c) Does 7 × 4 = (7 × 2) + (7 × 2) ?

(2)   Find the value of:

     (a)   3 × 10;   3 × (4 + 6);   (3 × 4) + (3 × 6)
     (b)   7 × 9;   7 × (5 + 4);   (7 × 5) + (7 × 4)
     (c)   4 × 16;   4 × (7 + 9);   (4 × 7) + (4 × 9)
     (d)   5 × 12;   5 × (10 + 2);   (5 × 10) + (5 × 2)
     (e)   10 × 13;   10 × (10 + 3);   (10 × 10) + (10 × 3)
     (f)   9 × 18;   9 × (10 + 8);   (9 × 10) + (9 × 8)
     (g)   6 × 22;   6 × (20 + 2);   (6 × 20) + (6 × 2)
     (h)   8 × 47;   8 × (40 + 7);   (8 × 40) + (8 × 7)

(3)   Examine the pattern of question (2) then copy and complete:

     (a)   2 × 24 = 2 × (20 + 4) = (2 × 20) + (×   )
     (b)   5 × 51 = 5 × (50 + 1) = (×   ) + (×   )
     (c)   10 × 83 = 10 × (+   ) = (×   ) + (×   )
     (d)   9 × 35 =   × (   ) = (   ) + (   )
     (e)   7 × 69 =   × (   ) = (   ) + (   )
     (f)   a × (b + c) = (   ) + (   )

The Distributive Law of Multiplication over Addition
If a, b and c are any three numbers, then
         a × (b + c) = (a × b) + (a × c) *or* a (b + c) = ab + ac
and   (a × b) + (a × c) = a × (b + c) *or* ab + ac = a(b + c)

Note: We may use the Distributive Law for the multiplication of number containing two or more digits.

Napier's Rods

A Calculating Aid

Many people such as Accountants, Bankers, Engineers, Scientists and Astronomers require to perform many long calculations daily in their work. Various aids have been invented through the years to reduce the time taken and also to prevent errors in calculation. John Napier (1550–1617) was a famous Scottish mathematician who invented two such aids — Logarithms and Rods.

Study this multiplication square

X	0	1	2	3	4	5	6	7	8	9
1	0	1	2	3	4	5	6	7	8	9
2	0	2	4	6	8	1/0	1/2	1/4	1/6	1/8
3	0	3	6	9	1/2	1/5	1/8	2/1	2/4	2/7
4	0	4	8	1/2	1/6	2/0	2/4	2/8	3/2	3/6
5	0	5	1/0	1/5	2/0	2/5	3/0	3/5	4/0	4/5
6	0	6	1/2	1/8	2/4	3/0	3/6	4/2	4/8	5/4
7	0	7	1/4	2/1	2/8	3/5	4/2	4/9	5/6	6/3
8	0	8	1/6	2/4	3/2	4/0	4/8	5/6	6/4	7/2
9	0	9	1/8	2/7	3/6	4/5	5/4	6/3	7/2	8/1

Note:

The diagonal divides each square into two parts thus, and .

The ten's digit is entered top-left of the diagonal and the unit's digit is entered bottom-right of the diagonal.

To make a set of Napier's Rods:

- (a) Cut out a rectangular card 11 cm by 10 cm.

- (b) Divide the card into centimetre squares.

- (c) Copy the diagonals and numbers exactly as shown in the multiplication square above.

- (d) Cut along the lines indicated by the arrows.

Multiplication using Napier's Rods

To find 3 × 28 and 8 × 28, select the
rods headed X, 2 and 8 placing
them together as shown.

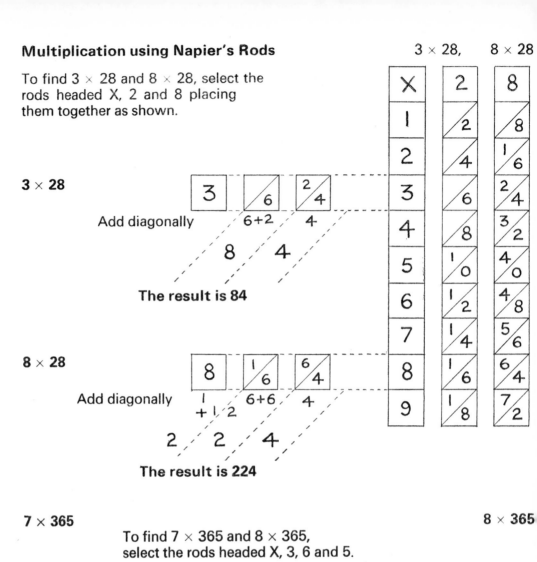

3 × 28

Add diagonally   6+2   4

8   4

The result is 84

8 × 28

Add diagonally   6+6   4

1 + 1 2

2   2   4

The result is 224

7 × 365

To find 7 × 365 and 8 × 365,
select the rods headed X, 3, 6 and 5.

8 × 365

Add diagonally

2   5   5   5

Add diagonally

2   9   2   0

7 × 365 = 2 555

8 × 365 = 2 920

Using the Rods, find the answers to:

(1) 4 × 67	(2) 3 × 24	(3) 5 × 47	(4) 8 × 59	(5) 7 × 68
(6) 2 × 581	(7) 3 × 487	(8) 6 × 753	(9) 7 × 753	(10) 9 × 803
(11) 4 × 35	(12) 9 × 23	(13) 8 × 64	(14) 6 × 64	(15) 4 × 79
(16) 3 × 682	(17) 4 × 251	(18) 7 × 529	(19) 8 × 529	(20) 8 × 749

36

Multiplication by Two digit numbers using Napiers' Rods   37 × 596

37 × 596

Select the rods headed X, 5, 9 and 6

Since 3 × 596 = 1 788

I   7   8   8

30 × 596 = 17 880

and   7 × 596 = 4 172

so   37 × 596 = 22 052

4   I   7   2

The result is 22 052

Using the Rods, find the answers to:

37

(1) 25 × 39   (2) 61 × 54   (3) 47 × 56   (4) 38 × 38   (5) 53 × 64

(6) 52 × 168   (7) 27 × 693 (8) 69 × 854 (9) 44 × 790 (10) 87 × 689

Assignment: Find out about the following aids to calculation:

Japanese Abacus, Logarithmic Tables, Slide Rule, Desk Calculator and *Computer.*

What are these aids?

Where do you find them?

Who uses them?

Why is $10^2 \times 10^3 = 10^5$ and why is this connected with logarithms?

Averages

A pupil's marks in 5 tests are
7, 9, 6, 8 and 5
Find his average mark per test.

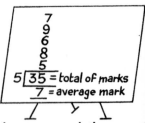

Note: 'Average mark = 7' means that the pupil would have scored the same total of marks if he had scored 7 in each test.

That is, Total of marks $= 7 + 7 + 7 + 7 + 7$
$= 5 \times 7$
$=$ (number of tests) $\times$ (average mark)

That is, Average mark $= \dfrac{\text{Total of marks}}{\text{Number of tests}}$

or, $A = \dfrac{T}{N}$

38

(1) Find the average of 297, 308, 279, 301, 310, 275.

(2) Find the average of 13·75, 9·07, 10·6, 12·54.

(3) The number of pulse beats per minute of a hospital patient is checked and the following readings recorded: 87, 89, 85, 80, 74, 82, 84. Find the average pulse rate per minute.

(4) In an examination the top 9 pupils score the following marks: 495, 489, 488, 483, 482, 478, 478, 476, 469. Find the average of these marks per pupil.

(5) In five successive weeks a boy earns £2·63, £1·96, £2·07, 84p and £1·60. Find the average weekly amount earned.

(6) A car laps a racing circuit in the following times, 97·8 sec, 96·6 sec, 98·3 sec, 99·4 sec, 94·9 sec. Find the average time for the circuit.

(7) One side of an L.P. record has six songs. They run for the following times: 3 min 9 sec, 2 min 59 sec, 3 min 6 sec, 2 min 15 sec, 2 min 2 sec, 2 min 29 sec. Find the average running time per song.

(8) The total number of pupils in a school is 455. If there are 13 classes find the average number of pupils per class.

(9) Mother spends a total of £12·95 in one week on food. Find the average amount spent per day.

(10) Dad uses a total of 1 092 litres of petrol per year. Find the average amount of petrol used (a) per week, (b) per day.

(11) Mother's total bill for electricity for a year is £44·72. Find the average cost of electricity per week.

Assignments

(1) Each pupil in the class should find out his or her own weight in kilo-grammes.   Find the average weight of the pupils in your class.

(2) Similarly find the average height of the pupils in your class (use centi-metres).

(3) Similarly find the average age of the pupils in your class (years, months).

(4) Read the outside temperature at the same time each day for a week. Using strips of coloured paper make a column graph showing this information.   At the end of the week calculate the average daily temperature.

(5) Find from a local newspaper the number of hours of sunshine in your district each day for a week. Draw a column graph showing this informa-tion.   Calculate the average number of hours of sunshine per day, over that week.

(6) Using newspaper information as in question (5) find the average rainfall per day in your district, over a period of 30 days.

Given the average value per item, find the total value

Using the notation on page 34

$$T = N \times A$$

39

(1) A pupil scores an average mark of 63 in 9 tests.   Find the total of his marks for these tests.

(2) At a certain point on a busy road the average number of vehicles passing is 42 per minute.   Calculate the total number of vehicles passing per hour.

(3) An average of 65p is spent by 180 customers in a butcher's shop.   What is the total amount spent by them in this shop?

(4) A man walks an average of 32 kilometres per day.   How far does he walk in 25 days?

(5) An electric radiator burns an average of 6 hours per day.   What is the total number of hours the radiator burns in 365 days?

(6) The average cost of running a car is £3·65 per week.   What is the total cost for a year?

(7) The average number of runs scored by seven batsmen in a cricket match is 62.   If six of the batsmen scored 103, 89, 0, 51, 23 and 32 runs respectively, what was the seventh batsman's score?

(8) The average weight of passengers in a plane is 63·7 kg. Find the total weight of passengers if the plane holds 150.

(9) A shop serves an average of 2 customers every 15 minutes. What is the total number of customers served in a 10-hour day?

(10) The average number of people to one square kilometre in Scotland is about 67. If the area of Scotland is taken as 77 000 square kilometres find the approximate population of Scotland.

(11) If in England the average number of people to one square kilometre is 337 and the area is 128 000 square kilometres, find the approximate population of England.

(12) Abe says that his family eat an average of 400 grammes of meat per day. Find the number of kilogrammes of meat they eat per year (365 days).

(13) If Glasgow has an average of 445 pupils in each of 399 schools, find the total number of pupils in these schools.

Using the notation on page 34

$$N = \frac{T}{A}$$

40

(1) A pupil's average mark is 29 for a series of monthly tests. If the total of his marks is 203, find the number of tests.

(2) The total of attendances for a number of games at a football ground is 79 200. The average attendance per game is 3 600. Find the number of games.

(3) National Parks in England occupy a total area of 5 810 km². If the average size of a park is 830 km², find the number of National Parks in England.

(4) Father's average electricity bill is £15 per quarter. If he pays a total of £450 over a certain time, how many bills does he pay?

(5) The National Health Service provides a total of half-a-million beds in hospitals. The average number of beds per hospital is 160. Find the number of hospitals.

(6) A litre of paint covers an average of 8·4 square metres. How many litres are required for a total area of 63 square metres?

Areas and Nets

AREA

Square

Rectangle
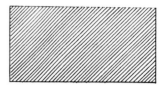

41

Assignment 1:

Draw a square of side 2 cm and a rectangle 4 cm long by 2 cm wide.

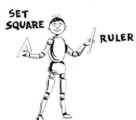
SET
SQUARE
RULER

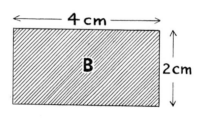
Rectangle

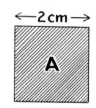
Square

Copy and complete:

(a) The area of Square A is ☐ cm².

(b) The area of Rectangle B is ☐ cm².

(c) The sides of a square are ———— —— length.

(d) The opposite sides of a rectangle are ———— —— length.

Assignment 2:

Make a tracing of your rectangle B.

Tracing Paper

(a) Does your tracing *always* fit exactly onto your rectangle?

(b) What is the area of your rectangle?

(c) What is the area of your rectangle placed in any position?

(d) If you cut your rectangle into two pieces what would be the *total area* of these two pieces?

(e) If the rectangle was divided into ten pieces what would be the total area of these ten pieces?

Assignment 3:

Make a tracing of your square A.

(a) Does the tracing *always* fit exactly onto your square?

(b) What is the area of your square when it is placed in any position?

(c) If you were to cut your square into four pieces what would be the **total area of these four pieces?**

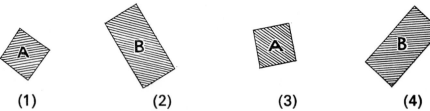

(1)　　　　(2)　　　　(3)　　　　(4)

These are different positions of Square A and Rectangle B.

(d) Copy and complete this Table:

Figure	Shape	Area (cm²)
1		
2		
3		
4		

ABE JUGGLES SHAPES

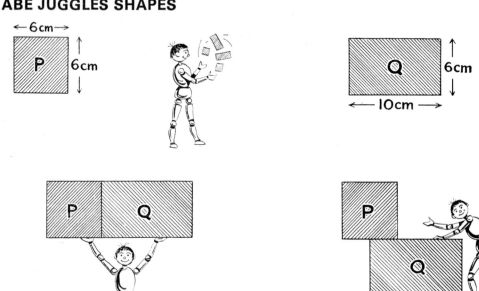

Figure (i)　　　　　　Figure (ii)

Find the total of Abe's areas in:

Figure (i) and Figure (ii)

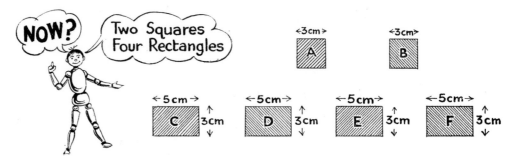

42

(1) Copy and complete:

    (a) Shape A = Shape ☐ in area.

    (b) Shape C = Shape ☐ or ☐ or ☐ in area.

    (c) Shape F = Shape ☐ or ☐ or ☐ in area.

(2) Find:

    (a) The area of this shape

    (b) The area of this shape

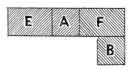

(3) Find the area of this shape:

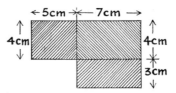

(4) Find the area of the shaded part of this figure

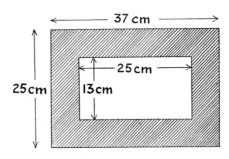

(5) A room is 4 metres long by 3·35 metres wide. How many square metres of carpet are needed to cover the floor?

(6) If the room in (5) is covered with carpet at £4·85/m² what is the cost if the customer must purchase complete square metres of carpet?

(7) A rectangular lawn is 12 m long by 6 m broad. One kilogramme of grass seed cost 53p. What will be the cost of resowing the lawn if one kilogramme of seed is needed for 2 square metres of lawn?

NETS

Abe makes a net of squares and rectangles.

> **P** represents a square
> **R** represents a rectangle

43

(1) How many rectangles are labelled in Abe's net?
(2) How many squares are labelled in Abe's net?
(3) **Assignment:** Make a net like Abe's. You will need **four** rectangles of equal area and having the same dimensions, as well as two equal squares whose sides are equal in length to one of the sides of the rectangle.

　(a) Fold your net at the edges of the central 'P-shape'.

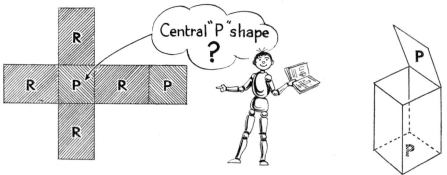

　(b) What common object can be made with this net?

Assignment: Make a closed box 5 cm long, 3 cm wide and 4 cm high.
(4) Make a net of rectangles as shown below.

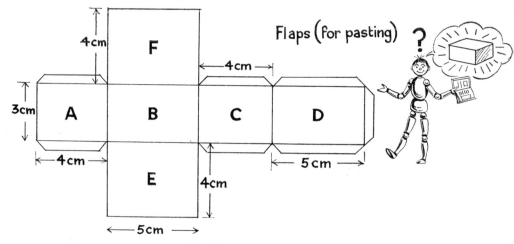

Note: The flaps may be pasted or gummed.

(5) Using the net you made in (4), make a box like Abe's.

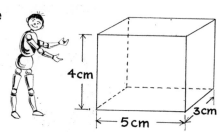

(6) Copy and complete this Table for Abe's net:

Shape	Area
A	12 cm^2
B	
C	
D	
E	
F	

(7) What area of cardboard was required to make your box? (Do not include the flaps).

(8) Abe **cuts** along the edges of a closed cardboard box.

    (a) How many rectangles did he get?

    (b) How many pairs of rectangles, equal in area, did Abe find?

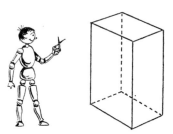

Abe has Information

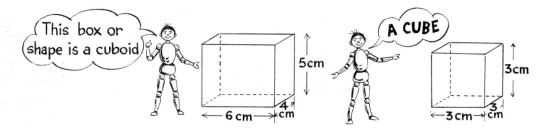

(9) How does a cube differ from a cuboid?

> Remember:
> A Cube and a Cuboid each have six faces.

ABE HAS A PROBLEM

How much cardboard is needed to make a closed box 3cm by 4cm by 7cm?

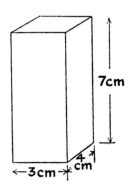

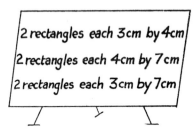

2 rectangles each 3cm by 4cm

2 rectangles each 4cm by 7cm

2 rectangles each 3cm by 7cm

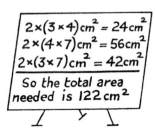

$2 \times (3 \times 4)\,cm^2 = 24\,cm^2$

$2 \times (4 \times 7)\,cm^2 = 56\,cm^2$

$2 \times (3 \times 7)\,cm^2 = 42\,cm^2$

So the total area needed is 122 cm²

44

(1) How much cardboard is needed to make a cuboid 10 cm long, 8 cm wide and 2 cm high? (Make no allowance for pasting flaps.)

Complete: The total area required is:

$2 \times (10 \times 8)\ cm^2 + 2 \times (10 \times 2)\ cm^2 + 2 \times (8 \times 2)\ cm^2$

$= \square\ cm^2 + \square\ cm^2 + \square\ cm^2$

$= \square\ cm^2$

(2) A cube has an *edge* 4 cm long. What area of cardboard (excluding the flaps) is needed to make it?

(3) A wooden box is *cuboidal* in shape and without a lid. The external dimensions are 15 cm by 10 cm by 20 cm. The wood is $\frac{1}{2}$ cm thick. How much wood $\frac{1}{2}$ cm thick is required to make this box?

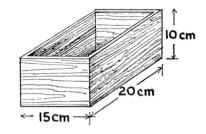

(4) The *edge* of a cardboard cube is 5 cm in length. Allowing 9 cm² of cardboard for the 'pasting flaps', calculate how much cardboard is required to make it.

> The Surface Area of a cube or cuboid is the
> Total of the Areas of its faces.

(5) Find the total surface area for each of these cubes or cuboids:
- (a) 2 cm by 3 cm by 4 cm
- (b) 4 cm by 3 cm by 5 cm
- (c) 20 cm by 5 cm by 10 cm
- (d) 15 cm by 3 cm by 12 cm
- (e) 4 cm by 4 cm by 4 cm
- (f) 17 cm by 17 cm by 17 cm
- (g) 21 cm by 10 cm by 20 cm
- (h) 25 cm by 4 cm by 8 cm
- (i) 8 m by 9 m by 8 m
- (j) 11 m by 12 m by 6 m
- (k) 2·5 m by 2 m by 1·5 m
- (l) 4·2 m by 5 m by 3 m
- (m) 3·5 cm by 2·5 cm by 4 cm
- (n) 6·5 cm by 1·2 cm by 5 cm
- (o) 40 m by 50 m by 10 m
- (p) 12·5 m by 8 m by 2·35 m

ABE'S MIXED BAG

45

(1) What is the area of a table top 1·5 m wide and 2 m long?

(2) A cricket wicket is 20 m long and 3 m wide. What is the area of the wicket?

(3) 0·5 litre of varnish covers 1·5 square metres. How many litres would be required to varnish the table top in (1)?

(4) What is the area of grass on a football pitch 100 m long and 60 m wide? What is the cost of returfing this pitch at 55 p/m²?

(5) A metal cube has an edge of 2 m. What is its surface area?

(6) What is the total surface area of a closed chocolate box 3 cm high, 10 cm wide and 18 cm long?

(7) A water tank, cuboidal in shape, is 12 m long, 8 m wide and 6 m high, what is its total surface area? (Tank is open at top.) What is the cost of coating the outside of this tank at £1·95/m²? The tank rests on a concrete base.

(8) One litre of a certain paint covers 2 m² and costs 32p. What is the cost of painting the outside of a metal cuboidal container 12 m × 3·5 m × 6·5 m? The container is open at one end.

(9) A hollow box cuboidal in shape is made of wood 1cm thick. The outside dimensions are 10 cm × 18 cm × 12 cm. If this box is closed what is:
- (a) the total external surface area of the box?
- (b) the total internal surface area of the box?
- (c) the volume of wood in the box?

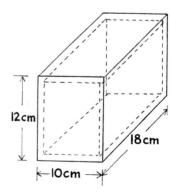

12cm

18cm

10cm

Perimeter

Farmer Abe has a field to be fenced!

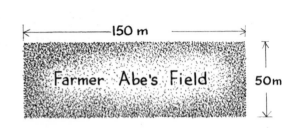

46

(1) (a) What shape is Farmer Abe's field?
   (b) State the lengths of the sides of his field.
   (c) What is the sum of the lengths of the four sides of this field?
   (d) What length of fencing is required to enclose this field completely?
   (e) If two gates each 3 m long are inserted in the fencing how much fencing is now required?

   Abe says:

The *perimeter* of a rectangular field is the sum of the lengths of its four sides.

   (f) What is the perimeter of Farmer Abe's field?

(2) Calculate the perimeter of a rectangular field measuring 45 m by 32 m.

(3) Find the perimeter of a rectangular estate 725·5 m long and 334·4 m broad. What length of fencing is required to enclose this estate if 8 gates each 3·5 m long are required in the perimeter?

(4) In a garden there are 4 rectangular flower beds each 3 m by 2·5 m. Find the total of the perimeters of these flower beds.

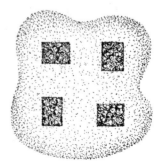

(5) A room is 5 m by 4 m. A strip of linoleum, 30 cm wide, is to be laid around the room as a border. What length of linoleum is required?

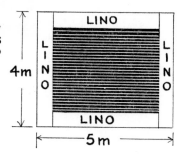

(6) Abe has a 'net' of rectangles as shown below:

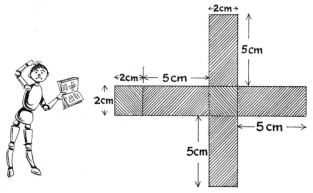

(a) What 3 dimensional shape can be constructed with this net?
(b) What is the perimeter of Abe's net?
(c) What is the sum of the lengths of the edges of the 3 dimensional shape which Abe has made with this net?

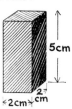

The Triangle

ABE'S NEW SHAPE

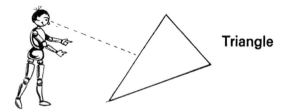

Triangle

47

(1) How many sides form the perimeter of this figure?

(2) What name is given to this figure?

(3) If the three sides of a triangle are 4 cm, 6 cm and 8 cm in length, find its perimeter.

(4) Abe draws another figure. What is the perimeter of Abe's figure?

(5) Find the perimeter of a triangle whose sides are 17·5 cm, 8·5 cm and 14·5 cm long.

(6) (a) What is the perimeter of a rectangle 15 cm long and 5 cm broad?
(b) If the length is increased by 10% and the breadth by 20% what is the new perimeter of the rectangle?

(7) A triangular plot is to be fenced with railing at a cost of 50 p/metre. The sides of the plot are 20·5 m, 30·5 m and 20·5 m in length. How much will this railing cost?

(8) Find the perimeter of a triangle having sides of length 112·5 cm, 82·7 cm and 54·3 cm.

(9) A sailing race is to take place on a triangular course marked by three buoys. If the distances between the buoys are 10·5 km, 10·8 km and 19·5 km what is the length of the course?

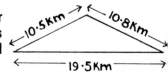

Binary Numbers

When we count in TENS using the set of symbols {0, 1, 2, 3, 4, 5, 6, 7, 8, 9 } we are using the DENARY or TENS system, thus:

$$4\,932 = 4 \text{ thousands} + 9 \text{ hundreds} + 3 \text{ tens} + 2 \text{ units}$$
$$= (4 \times 1\,000) + (9 \times 100) + (3 \times 10) + (2 \times 1)$$
$$= (4 \times 10^3) + (9 \times 10^2) + (3 \times 10^1) + (2 \times 1)$$

> $7 \times 10^3 + 8 \times 10^2 + 3 \times 10^1 + 4$
> $= 7 \times 1000 + 8 \times 100 + 3 \times 10 + 4$
> $= 7000 + 800 + 30 + 4$
> $= 7\,834$

48

Write the denary numbers represented in the following table:

	10^4	10^3	10^2	10^1	UNITS
(1)		7	8	3	4
(2)		2	7	5	6
(3)	2	0	5	3	1
(4)	9	3	6	0	5
(5)	8	4	2	6	9

There are other ways of counting. One of these is the BINARY System in which only two symbols are used to represent any number.

When we count in TWOS using only the set of symbols {0, 1 } we are using the BINARY System.

Binary place values corresponding to the denary place values above are:

2^4	2^3	2^2	2^1	UNITS

> Powers of Two
> $2^4 = 2 \times 2 \times 2 \times 2$
> $= \underline{16}$

These place values are:

$$2^1 = 2 \qquad\qquad = 2$$
$$2^2 = 2 \times 2 \qquad\quad = 4$$
$$2^3 = 2 \times 2 \times 2 \qquad = 8$$
$$2^4 = 2 \times 2 \times 2 \times 2 = 16$$

What binary number is shown in this table?

2^4	2^3	2^2	2^1	UNITS
1	0	1	1	1

The binary number 10111 represents:

$$1 \times 2^4 + 0 \times 2^3 + 1 \times 2^2 + 1 \times 2^1 + 1 \times 1$$
$$= 1 \times 16 + 0 \times 8 + 1 \times 4 + 1 \times 2 + 1 \times 1$$
$$= 16 + 0 + 4 + 2 + 1$$
$$= 23$$

So the binary number 10111 represents 23 in the denary or tens system.

This binary number, 10111, is read as 'one-zero-one-one-one'.

Write the tens or denary numbers 0, 1, 2, 3, 4, ..., ..., ..., ..., 9, 10 as binary numbers:

Denary or Tens System		Binary System	2^3	2^2	2^1	1
0 =	0	0×1				0
1 =	1	1×1				1
2 =	2 + 0	$1 \times 2^1 + 0 \times 1$			1	0
3 =	2 + 1	$1 \times 2^1 + 1 \times 1$			1	1
4 =	4 + 0 + 0	$1 \times 2^2 + 0 \times 2^1 + 0 \times 1$		1	0	0
5 =	4 + 0 + 1	$1 \times 2^2 + 0 \times 2^1 + 1 \times 1$		1	0	1
6 =	4 + 2 + 0	$1 \times 2^2 + 1 \times 2^1 + 0 \times 1$		1	1	0
7 =	4 + 2 + 1	$1 \times 2^2 + 1 \times 2^1 + 1 \times 1$		1	1	1
8 = 8 + 0 + 0 + 0		$1 \times 2^3 + 0 \times 2^2 + 0 \times 2^1 + 0 \times 1$	1	0	0	0
9 = 8 + 0 + 0 + 1		$1 \times 2^3 + 0 \times 2^2 + 0 \times 2^1 + 1 \times 1$	1	0	0	1
10 = 8 + 0 + 2 + 0		$1 \times 2^3 + 0 \times 2^2 + 1 \times 2^1 + 0 \times 1$	1	0	1	0

So,

Denary Numbers	0	1	2	3	4	5	6	7	8	9	10
Binary Numbers	0	1	10	11	100	101	110	111	1000	1001	1010

(1) Write the denary numbers 11, 12, 13, ..., ..., ..., ..., 19, 20 as binary numbers.

(2) Write the next three members of the sequence:

2, 4, 8, 16, ..., ..., ...

(3) Copy and complete the sequence:
$$2^8, 2^7, 2^6, 2^5, 2^4, 2^3, 2^2, \ldots, \ldots$$

(4) Copy and complete the following table:

	$2^6=64$	$2^5=32$	$2^4=16$	$2^3=8$	$2^2=4$	$2^1=2$	Units	Denary Number
(a)					1	1	1	$4+2+1=7$
(b)			1	1	1	0	0	$16+8+4=28$
(c)			1	0	1	0	1	
(d)			1	1	0	1	0	
(e)		1	1	0	0	1	1	
(f)		1	0	1	0	0	1	
(g)	1	0	1	1	0	1	0	
(h)	1	1	0	0	1	1	0	

(5) Write the following binary numbers as denary numbers:

    (a)   11101   (b)   101011   (c)   100011

    (d)   101110   (e) 1110010   (f) 1101010

    (g) 1010101   (h) 1101101   (i) 1001010

$$101010$$
$$= 1 \times 2^5 + 0 \times 2^4 + 1 \times 2^3 + 0 \times 2^2 + 1 \times 2^1 + 0 \times 1$$
$$= 32 + 0 + 8 + 0 + 2 + 0$$
$$= 32 + 8 + 2$$
$$= \underline{42}$$

DENARY NUMBERS TO BINARY NUMBERS

The following example demonstrates how denary numbers may be readily converted into binary numbers:

(1)

2	37
2	18, **1**
2	9, **0**
2	4, **1**
2	2, **0**
2	1, **0**
	0, **1**

Divide 37 by 2 to get 18 remainder **1**
Divide 18 by 2 to get 9 remainder **0**
Divide 9 by 2 to get 4 remainder **1**
Divide 4 by 2 to get 2 remainder **0**
Divide 2 by 2 to get 1 remainder **0**
Divide 1 by 2 to get 0 remainder **1**

Read the remainders from bottom to top, and write them from left to right to form the required binary number.

$$37 = 100101$$

Here are three further conversions to study:

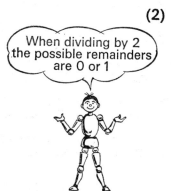

When dividing by 2 the possible remainders are 0 or 1

(2)

2	94
2	47, 0
2	23, 1
2	11, 1
2	5, 1
2	2, 1
2	1, 0
	0, 1

(3)

2	100
2	50, 0
2	25, 0
2	12, 1
2	6, 0
2	3, 0
2	1, 1
	0, 1

(4)

2	367
2	183, 1
2	91, 1
2	45, 1
2	22, 1
2	11, 0
2	5, 1
2	2, 1
2	1, 0
	0, 1

$$94 = \mathbf{1011110}$$ $$100 = \mathbf{1100100}$$ $$367 = \mathbf{101101111}$$

Convert the following denary numbers to binary numbers:

(1) 20 (2) 29 (3) 34 (4) 39 (5) 49 (6) 73
(7) 99 (8) 110 (9) 144 (10) 250 (11) 350 (12) 500

The worked examples above may be checked by entering the binary numbers in a table as follows:

	256	128	64	32	16	8	4	2	UNITS	DENARY NUMBER
(1)				1	O	O	1	O	1	37
(2)			1	O	1	1	1	1	O	94
(3)			1	1	O	O	1	O	O	100
(4)	1	O	1	1	O	1	1	1	1	367

For example, from the table, the fourth number gives:

$1 \times 256 + 0 \times 128 + 1 \times 64 + 1 \times 32 + 0 \times 16 + 1 \times 8 + 1 \times 4 + 1 \times 2 + 1 \times 1$
$= 256 + 0 + 64 + 32 + 0 + 8 + 4 + 2 + 1$
$= 256 + 64 + 32 + 8 + 4 + 2 + 1$
$= 367$

So, **101101111** in binary represents 367 in denary.

Draw a table like the one above and use it to check that the binary numbers you get in exercise 50 are correct.

FUN WITH BINARY NUMBERS

Assignment 1: Find out why the binary system of counting is important to the Computer Industry.

Assignment 2: Seven pupils in the class should each bring to school a torch which is working and be allowed to demonstrate binary numbers as follows:

Torch on represents 1   Torch off represents 0

As the lights are switched on or off at random, say ten times the remainder of the class record what they see thus:

(1) Write the binary numbers represented by the following

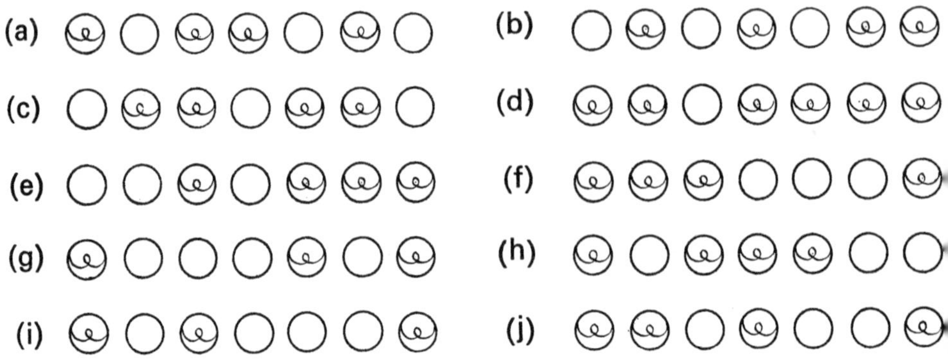

(a)   (b)

(c)   (d)

(e)   (f)

(g)   (h)

(i)   (j)

(2) Write in denary form the binary numbers in (1).

(3) Repeat (1) and (2) for a team of your classmates each with a torch and making their own binary numbers.

Progress Checks

PROGRESS CHECK 4

(1) Add: 3 172 + 586 + 2 943 + 7 364.

(2) Divide 5 032 by 37.

(3) Dad's wages in four successive weeks were £17·56, £23·10, £19·45 and £22·97. Find his average weekly wage.

(4) The total of marks scored by 35 pupils, in a class test, was 1 295. What was the average mark?

(5) Change the binary number 1011011 to a denary number.

(6) Write down the next three members of the sequence:
16, 8, 4, 2, 1, ..., ..., ...

(7) A field, rectangular in shape, is 25·5 m broad and 92·5 m long. Find the perimeter of the field.

(8) Find the perimeter of the figure shown in diagram.

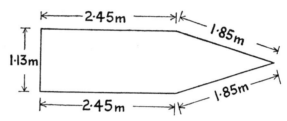

(9) The net of a cuboid consists of 4 rectangles, each 12 cm by 6 cm, and 2 squares of 6 cm side. What is the total surface area of the cuboid?

(10) A cuboid has dimensions 20 cm by 25 cm by 8 cm. What is the total surface area of the cuboid?

PROGRESS CHECK 5

(1) From 12 364 subtract 8 976.

(2) Find □: (96 × 74) + (96 × 26) = □.

(3) A tea merchant makes up 3 040 packets of tea and packs them into 124 boxes with 24 packets in each box. How many packets remain unpacked?

(4) Find, as a decimal, the average of 0, $\frac{1}{2}$, 0·81, 0·75, $\frac{7}{10}$ and 0·30.

(5) Change the denary number 156 to a binary number.

(6) The average weight of a 50p coin is 13·5 grammes. Find in kilogrammes the weight of four hundred 50p coins.

(7) The course of an aircraft race is in the shape of a triangle with sides of 210 km, 305 km and 406 km. If the race consists of four laps, find the total distance of the race.

(8) A container is in the shape of a cube of edge 3 metres. What would it cost to paint the whole outside of the container at £1·25/m²?

(9) A carpet 2·5 m by 3 m, is to be laid in a room 3 m by 3·5 m. What area of the floor will not be carpeted?

PROGRESS CHECK 6

(1) Find the value of 326×84.

(2) Find the replacement for $\square$: $(637 \div 13) + (19 \times 17) = \square$

(3) A boy scored a total of 295 marks in an examination. If his average mark was 59, how many tests did he sit?

(4) A man who smoked 15 cigarettes a day stopped smoking. How much did he save altogether in February and March, 1971, when his cigarettes would have cost him 30p for 20?

(5) Express the sum of the binary numbers 1010 and 101010 as a number to base 10 (denary).

(6) A farmer has to fence a rectangular field, the sides of which are 33·8 m and 77·6 m in length. If two gates 3·4 m wide are to be fitted, what length of fencing is required?

(7) Find the area of a rectangle 3·3 m long and 2·5 m broad.

(8) How many square centimetres of a certain wood are required to make a box 23 cm long, 12 cm broad and 8 cm high? The box has no lid.

Profit and Loss

PROFIT AND LOSS

Abe buys 20 stamps for 6p.

Abe sells the stamps for 10p

Thus Abe's profit is 4p.

In the stamp shop   Next day at school

A *Profit* is made when the total Sales are greater than the total Expenditure.
A *Loss* is made when the total Sales are less than the total Expenditure.
Profit/Loss is the difference between the total Sales and the total Expenditure.

A school buys 200 packets of crisps for £4·62 and sells them at 3p per packet. Find the profit.

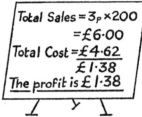

Total Sales = 3p × 200
= £6·00
Total Cost = £4·62
£1·38
The profit is £1·38

53

(1) A man bought a picture for £10. Find his profit on selling the picture for £12·50.

(2) The sales of crisps in Centre School total £2·88. If the crisps cost £2·21, what is the profit?

(3) Find the profit in selling a supply of crisps for £28·80 if the cost was £21·61.

(4) Mother bought a new pair of shoes for £2·25. The shoes did not fit and could not be returned since they were bought at a 'sale'. She sold the shoes for £1·50. How much did she lose?

(5) A boy bought a second-hand bicycle for £7·20. Find his loss on selling the bicycle for £5·65.

(6) A school buys a carton of crisps containing 48 packets for £1·15 and sells the crisps at 3p per packet. Find the profit to the School Fund.

(7) What is the total profit on selling 144 packets of crisps at 3p per packet if the total cost is £3·30?

(8) In making a table, Tom spent 85p on wood, 4p on nails, 15p on glue and 17p on varnish. He sold the table for £1·50. How much did he gain or lose?

(9) The cost of making 42 bars of tablet for a Sale of Work is 86p. Find the total profit if each bar is sold at 4p.

(10) For the Sale of Work mother made 5 aprons from 2·5 metres of cloth at 30p per metre, 5 metres of binding at 6p per metre and 2 reels of cotton at 8p each. Find the total profit if the aprons were sold at 35p each.

OVERHEADS

Shopkeepers have many expenses in 'keeping a shop'. Rent, rates, wages, fittings, transport, insurance, electricity, telephone have to be paid for. Such expenses are called *Overheads*. Almost all business transactions incur overheads.

54

(1) What are the overheads of a grocer with a yearly wage bill of £3 025 if the upkeep of his shop costs an extra £2 483 ?

(2) The overheads of an agent were as follows: car, £576; store, £127·40; extras, £56·85. Find his total overheads.

(3) During a year the owner of a dairy noted that his expenses were as follows: rent and rates, £128; wages, £1 245; other expenses, £219. Find the total of these overheads.

(4) A hairdresser calculates that his annual overheads are: rates, £96; fittings and decoration, £286; gas and electricity, £105; wages and stamps, £4 285; other, £47·50. Find the total overheads.

(5) The annual expenses of an antique dealer were as follows: shop, £306; transport and insurance, £572·20; telephone, £73·65. What are the total overheads if his remaining expenses amount to £32·55 ?

Do you remember Abe buying 20 stamps for 6p and selling them for 10p? It appeared that Abe made a *profit* of 4p on this transaction.

If, however, it costs Abe 7p on bus fares to travel to the stamp shop then his total expenditure is 6p + 7p or 13p. The sales are 10p. Thus Abe makes a *loss* of 3p on selling the stamps.

Note: In the above example, the overheads are 7p.

During a certain year, the total sales of a shopkeeper amounted to £11 646 and the total purchases were £9 872. If his overheads were £915, find his profit.

Total Sales = £11 646
Total Expenditure £9 872 + £915
= £10 787
Profit = Sales − Expenditure
= £859
The profit was £859

55   Find the annual profit of each of the following shopkeepers:

	Type	Total Purchases	Total Sales	Overheads
(1)	Butcher	£12 924	£18 425	£3 263
(2)	Fruiterer	£6 642	£8 560	£484
(3)	Ironmonger	£18 786	£26 364	£5 427
(4)	Newsagent	£15 926	£21 489	£3 682
(5)	Hairdresser	£358	£5 025	£3 422
(6)	City Outfitter	£51 976	£92 584	£36 272
(7)	Grocer	£15 392	£19 054	£1 589
(8)	House Furnisher	£14 238	£22 315	£4 897
(9)	Boutique Owner	£4 827	£9 512	£1 826
(10)	Confectioner	£17 306	£21 614	£2 009

Note: In business it is usual to use the word *INCOME* instead of sales since income also includes fees, grants, interest . . . .

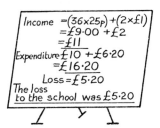

For a school outing, 36 pupils paid 25p each and 2 teachers paid £1 each. The hire of the bus was £10 and the other charges totalled £6·20. Find the loss to the school fund.

ABE'S BUSINESS METHOD

(a) Find the amount of all Sales or Income.
(b) Find the amount of all Expenditure.
(c) Compare Income with Expenditure and determine Profit or Loss.

56

(1) A man buys a second-hand car for £375 and spends £67 on improvements. Find his profit or loss on selling the car for £450.

(2) The sales of a milk vending machine amount to £46·04. Find the loss sustained if the milk cost £41·90 and the machine cost £5 to rent.

(3) The total income of a School Fund was £108. The expenses of the fund were £14·56, £18·39, £7·65 ,£36·92 and £16·76. Find the profit.

(4) The cost of hiring costumes for the School Concert was £14·80 and the other expenses totalled £6·65. The sales of tickets were £19·20 from adults and £6·05 from children. Find the profit to the school fund.

(5) The expenses of a Musical Club for the year were as follows: hire of rooms, electricity, etc., £46·50; teas, £7·25; stationery and postage, £5·15; Sundries, £2·96. If the income of the Club was £64 in subscriptions and £3·24 in bank interest, find the Club's profit for the year.

(6) The Income and Expenditure account of a golf club for a certain year was as follows:

INCOME			EXPENDITURE		
		£			£
Subscriptions	... ...	9 213	Course		6 107
Green Fees		490	Clubhouse		2 289
Rents		75	General		3 191
Interest		724	Competitions		737
Refreshments		2 356	Depreciation		1 207

Find the amount of the profit or of the loss.

(7) The total sales of a shopkeeper during a year were £22 647 and his total purchases were £14 568. If the overheads were £3 670 for wages, £1 256 for the upkeep of the shop and £1 325 for other expenses, find the profit for the year.

(8) A school milk-vending machine cost £5 per month to rent. Find the profit or the loss of the machine during a period of 6 months when the purchases of milk amounted to £298·50 and the sales totalled £337·65.

(9) The printer's bill for a school magazine was £104 and other expenses amounted to £8·20. If the school received donations totalling £22 and sold 536 magazines at 15p each, find the loss to the school fund from the magazine account.

(10) The average monthly sales of a kiosk are £826 and the average monthly costs of purchases are £638. Find the owners' annual profit if the overheads for the year total £479.

Foreign Exchange

FOREIGN CURRENCY

COUNTRY	STANDARD UNIT	RATE/£1
Belgium	Franc	120 Fr
France	Franc	13 Fr
Germany	Deutsche Mark	8·7 DM
Italy	Lira	1500 Lire
Portugal	Escudo	68 Esc
Spain	Peseta	170 P'tas
Switzerland	Franc	10·3 Fr
United States of America	Dollar	2·4 $

The table shows the approximate rates of exchange of certain foreign currencies (money) on 1st January, 1971. The standard unit of money in the United Kingdom is One Pound Sterling.

Each country issues its own money.

Note: The Belgian franc, the French franc and the Swiss franc have different values.

A British tourist spent Easter in Paris.

   (a) How many francs did she receive in exchange for £25?

   (b) What was the value in £ of a gift costing 33·80 francs?

Use the rates of exchange quoted in the table above.

   (1) Change:

     (a) £6 into Belgian francs   (b) £5 into Italian lire.

     (c) £8 into U.S.A. dollars   (d) £7 into Swiss francs.

     (e) £10 into Portuguese currency.   (f) £4·80 into Spanish currency.

     (g) £9·40 into German currency.   (h) £12·30 into French currency.

57

(2) Change into British currency:

    (a) 12 U.S.A. dollars   (b) 6 000 lire

    (c) 104 French francs   (d) 92·70 Swiss francs.

    (e) 238 escudos.   (f) 876 Belgian **francs.**

    (g) 1 088 pesetas.   (h) 53·07 DM.

(3) A business man exchanged £32 in Rome. How many lire did he obtain ?

(4) Margaret spent a holiday in Spain. She changed £9 into Spanish money and spent 1 480 pesetas. How many pesetas had she left at the end of her holiday ?

(5) A transistor in Portugal was priced at 894·20 Esc. How much is this in British currency ?

(6) At the end of his British tour, an American was left with £5·35. How much U.S.A. currency did he get in exchange ?

(7) Find, to the nearest 1p, the British exchange rate for 140 DM.

(8) Ronald spent a holiday in Belgium. He changed £20 into francs, spent 2 070 francs and converted the remaining francs into £. How much did he get in exchange ?

Scales and Plans

Here is a plan of a classroom floor.

Scale: 1 cm represents 1 metre.

(1) Measure in centimetres the length of the plan.

(2) Measure in centimetres the width of the plan.

(3) Using the **scale write** down the length and width of the classroom floor.

(4) Measure in centimetres the length of each of the following lines and use the **scale** indicated to find the measurement represented by each:
   (a) ———————————————— 1 cm represents 1 m.
   (b) ————————————————— 1 cm represents 2 m.
   (c) ——————————————— 1 cm represents 3 m.
   (d) ——————————————— 1 cm represents 4 m.
   (e) ———————————— 1 cm represents 10 m.
   (f) ————————————————— 1 cm represents 0·5 m.
   (g) —————————————— 1 cm represents 100 m.

   Assignment: Measure in metres the length and width of your classroom floor and draw a plan using a suitable scale.

(5) Using a scale of 1 cm to represent 10 m find the distances represented by lines with the following measurements:
   (a) 3 cm   (b) 15 cm   (c) 6·5 cm   (d) 10·5 cm
   (e) 14·5 cm   (f) 25·5 cm   (g) 7·25 cm   (h) 12·25 cm

(6) The length of a football pitch is 100 metres. Draw a line to represent this length using a scale of 1 cm to represent 10 metres.

(7) Using a scale of 1 cm to represent 5 m draw lines to represent:
   (a) 50 m   (b) 60 m   (c) 30 m   (d) 80 m
   (e) 45 m   (f) 75 m   (g) 55 m   (h) 25 m

(8) In a plan using a scale of 1 cm to represent 100 metres, what length of line would represent:
   (a) 200 m (b) 500 m (c) 1000 m (d) 2000 m (e) 5000 m (f) 250 m
   (g) 450 m (h) 650 m (i) 1200 m (j) 3400 m (k) 5450 m (l) 4350 m

This map shows some sea routes from England to the Continent:

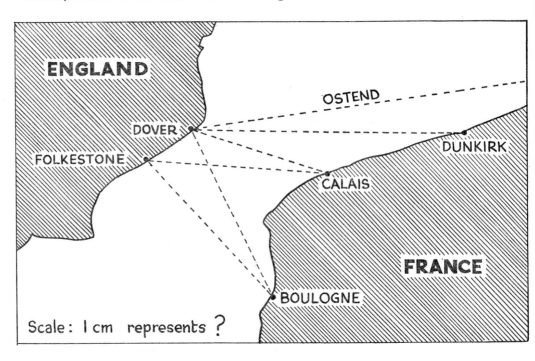

Scale: 1 cm represents ?

59

(1) Measure to the nearest half-centimetre the lines joining:.

    (a) Dover to Calais   (b) Dover to Boulogne

    (c) Dover to Dunkirk   (d) Folkstone to Calais

    (e) Folkestone to Boulogne

(2) The distance from Dover to Boulogne is 50 km. Find the scale of this map.

(3) Using this scale find the distance from:

    (a) Folkestone to Calais   (b) Dover to Calais

    (c) Dover to Dunkirk

(4) If the distance from Dover to Ostend is 110 km, what length of line would be required to join these points on a map with the same scale as the map above?

SCALE FACTOR

Scale: 1 cm represents 1 m ⟹ 1 cm on the diagram represents 1 m on the ground, or 1 cm on the diagram represents 100 cm on the ground.

The ratio of 1 to 100 is called the SCALE FACTOR of the diagram.

We write,　　　1 : 100 is the scale factor.

We read,　　　one to one hundred is the scale factor.

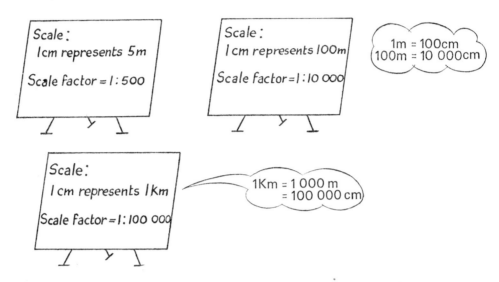

Note: Road Maps, Ordinance Survey maps, maps in an atlas and all plans indicate the scale used. Sometimes this is shown as a scale and sometimes as a scale factor.

60　　　(1)　Copy and complete the following table:

Scale	Scale Factor	Scale	Scale Factor
1 cm represents 0·25 km		1 cm represents 15 km	
1 cm represents 0·5 km		1 cm represents 20 km	
1 cm represents 1 km			1 : 4 000 000
1 cm represents 10 km	1 : 1 000 000		1 : 5 000 000
1 cm represents 5 km			1 : 10 000 000
1 cm represents 2·5 km		1 cm represents 200 km	

(2)　A map is marked with the scale factor 1 : 150 000. What distance in km is represented by 1 cm on the map?

(3)　The scale of a map is 1 cm represents 23·5 km. What is the scale factor of the map?

(4)　A pupil draws a plan of the school playing field using the scale 1 cm represents 15 m. What is the scale factor of the plan?

Assignment:　Draw a plan of the school playground or playing field using a suitable scale. Write the scale factor on the plan.

Volumes

VOLUME

Abe Drops a Brick

The jar was completely filled with water.

How much liquid was displaced?

Can you help Abe?

Clever Abe

← Measuring Jar

Abe's Brick

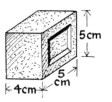

5 cm

5 cm

4 cm

The overflow of liquid in the measuring jar measures 100 cm³.

61

(1)   How much liquid did **Abe's brick** displace?

(2)   What object displaced **100 cm³** of liquid?

(3)   What is the displacement or **volume of Abe's brick?**

(4)   (a) What is $5 \times 4 \times 5$?   (b) What is 5 cm $\times$ 4 cm $\times$ 5 cm?

Abe examines his brick.

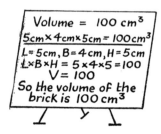

Volume = 100 cm³
5cm × 4cm × 5cm = 100cm³
L = 5cm, B = 4cm, H = 5cm
L × B × H = 5 × 4 × 5 = 100
V = 100
So the volume of the brick is 100 cm³

For any cuboid or rectangular solid,

Where L represents the measure or number of units of Length.

B represents the measure or number of units of Breadth.

H represents the measure or number of units of Height.

V represents the measure or number of units of Volume.

Then,

$$V = L \times B \times H$$

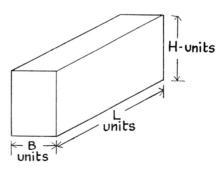

(5) Copy and complete the following:

The measure or number of units of Volume of a cube or cuboid is given by $V = \ldots \times \ldots \times \ldots$

> The measure, A, of the area of a rectangle is given by $L \times B$
> that is, $A = L \times B$.

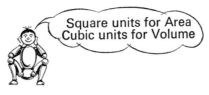

Abe says: Square units for Area, Cubic units for Volume.

62

(1) Find the replacements for ☐ in each of the following:

(a) $2\,cm \times 3\,cm = ☐\,cm^2$ (b) $2\,m \times 5\,m = ☐\,m^2$

(c) $2{\cdot}5\,cm \times 4\,cm = ☐\,cm^2$ (d) $4\,m \times 3{\cdot}5\,m = ☐\,m^2$

(2) Think! Copy and complete!

(a) $2\,cm \times 3\,cm \times 4\,cm = ☐\,cm^3$

(b) $6\,cm \times 5\,cm \times 4\,cm = 120\,☐$

(c) $5\,m \times 4\,m \times 7{\cdot}5\,m = ☐\,m^3$

(d) $12\,cm \times 5\,cm \times 4\,cm = ☐\,cm^3$

(3) You are calculating volume. What units are used?

(a) cm or cm^3 or cm^2 (b) m^2 or m or m^3

(4) You are calculating area. Which units are used?

(a) cm^2 or cm or cm^3 (b) m^2 or m^3 or m

Area   **Volume**

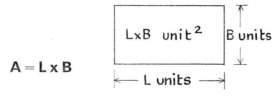

$A = L \times B$

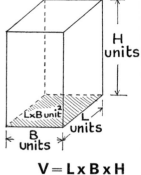

Abe's Code

L represents the measure or number of units of Length.

B represents the measure or number of units of Breadth.

H represents the measure or number of units of Height.

A represents the measure or number of units of Area.

V represents the measure or number of units of Volume.

$V = L \times B \times H$

or $V = A \times H$

VOLUMES (CUBES AND CUBOIDS)

Cube

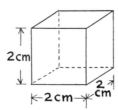

L = 2 cm, B = 2 cm, H = 2 cm

$2 \times 2 \times 2 = 8$

Cuboid

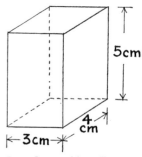

L = 4 cm, B = 3 cm, H = 5 cm

$4 \times 3 \times 5 = 60$

Says Abe, the Volume is:

$8 cm^3$ $60 cm^3$

63

(1) Find the volume of:

    (a) A cuboid of Length 20 cm, Breadth 4·5 cm and Height 12·5 cm

    (b) A cube of edge 8 cm

(2) A rectangular water tank measures 20 m in length, 15 m in breadth and 35 m in height. What is the volume of the tank?

(3)   (a) A water jar is completely filled with water. A brick, measuring 4 cm by 2 cm by 3 cm, is dropped into the jar. What volume of water is displaced?

    (b) If the jar held 100 cm³ of water, how much water does the jar hold after the brick has been dropped?

(4) Find the volume of a metal ingot which is 80 cm long, 12·5 cm broad and 6 cm high.

(5) The dimensions of a water tank are 17 cm by 12 cm by 25 cm. If a bucket holds 100 cm³ of water how many buckets, full of water, would be needed to fill the tank?

(6) How many cubes of edge 1 cm will fill a box measuring, internally, 12 cm by 20 cm by 15 cm?

(7) One cubic centimetre of aluminium weighs 2·70 g. What is the weight in grammes of a rectangular block of aluminium 50 cm long, 7·5 cm broad and 12 cm high?

(8) An iron bar is one metre long, 8 centimetres wide and 4 centimetres thick. What is the weight of this iron bar expressed in kilogrammes if it weighs 7·50 g/cm³?

(9) The diagram shows a metal block with a square hole of side 5 cm cut in it. If the metal weighs 3·75 gm/cm³ what is the weight of the block?

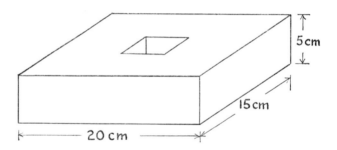

(10) Calculate the weight of metal in this alloy casting which has a square 'cross-section' and weighs 4·73 gm/cm³.

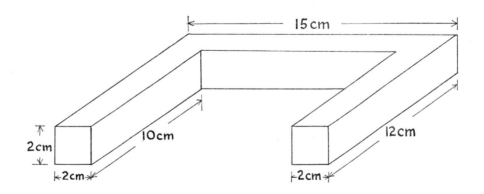

Metric Tonne

METRIC TONNE

334 563 kg
is equal to 334·563 tonnes (metric tonnes)

Abe Learns

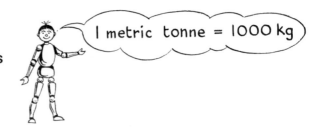

I metric tonne = 1000 kg

64

(1) How many kilogrammes are equivalent to 31 metric tonnes?

(2) 3 765·5 kgs is equivalent to how many metric tonnes?

(3) Change 89 754 kilogrammes to metric tonnes.

(4) Six lorries each weigh 4 650 kg when fully loaded. What is their total weight in tonnes?

(5) Find the cost of 36 metric tonnes of coal at £15·25/tonne.

(6) Eight rugby forwards have an average weight of 104 kg. What is their total weight in tonnes?

(7) 16 lorries have a total weight of 28 tonnes. If each lorry weighs exactly the same what will be the weight of one lorry?

(8) How many lorry loads will be required when moving 2 464 metric tonnes of vegetables if the lorry used can carry 16 metric tonnes?

(9) A steel casting is 500 cm long, 100 cm broad and 40 cm high. If the metal weighs 8 g/cc what is the weight in metric tonnes of this steel casting?

Mathematical Sentences

MATHEMATICAL SENTENCES

Find the replacement for the letter in each of the following so that these sentences are *true:*

65

(1) $3 + 7 = a$ (2) $9 + b = 11$ (3) $11 + c = 20$ (4) $d - 6 = 2$
(5) $21 - e = 9$ (6) $f - 4 = 9$ (7) $g + g = 18$ (8) $2h = 12$
(9) $5k = 35$ (10) $7m = 42$ (11) $10n = 90$ (12) $8p = 8$

(13) $q \div 3 = 5$ (14) $\dfrac{r}{6} = 3$ (15) $\dfrac{s}{10} = 4$ (16) $\dfrac{21}{t} = 7$

(17) $\dfrac{18}{u} = 2$ (18) $\dfrac{40}{v} = 5$ (19) $5 + w = 7 + 6$ (20) $4x = 60 + 20$

All the sentences above contain *is equal to* and so are called *equations.* The letters or unknowns in equations are called *variables.*

The *replacements* for the variables are often restricted to particular sets of numbers.

Example: If $x \in A$, where $A = \{1, 2, 3, 4, 5, 6, 7, 8, 9, 10\}$, find the replacement for x in each of the following equations so that they are true:

(a) $x + 7 = 10$ (b) $\frac{x}{5} = 3$

$$X + 7 = 10$$
$$X = 3$$
Since $3 \in A$, the replacement for X is 3

$$\frac{x}{5} = 3$$
$$X = 15$$
Since $15 \notin A$, there is no replacement for X

Find the replacements for the variables in each of the following equations so that they are true. The variables are members of the set A where $A = \{1, 2, 3, 4, 5, 6, 7, 8, 9, 10\}$:

66

(1) $2 + a = 11$ (2) $b - 1 = 4$ (3) $3c = 30$ (4) $d - 6 = 8$

(5) $\dfrac{e}{2} = 4$ (6) $\dfrac{27}{f} = 9$ (7) $5h = 100$ (8) $78 + k = 82$

(9) $w + w = 9$ (10) $\dfrac{22}{x} = 11$ (11) $3y = 36$ (12) $21 - z = 14$

Solution Sets

The set of replacements which make a mathematical sentence true is called the *solution set.*

To find the solution set (SS) is to solve the equation.

EQUATIONS

Solve: (a) $3a + 5 = 24$

(b) $18 - 5b = 3$

where the variables are members of the set of natural numbers.

$$3a + 5 = 24$$
$$\text{But } 19 + 5 = 24$$
$$\text{So} \quad 3a = 19$$
There is no natural number which makes this sentence true
$$SS = \{ \} \text{ or } \emptyset$$

$$18 - 5b = 3$$
$$\text{But } 18 - 15 = 3$$
$$\text{So} \quad 5b = 15$$
$$b = 3$$
$$SS = \{3\}$$

Solve the following equations where the variables are members of the set of natural numbers:

67

(1) $2c + 6 = 10$

(2) $3d + 5 = 14$

(3) $7 + 4e = 31$

(4) $2 + 5m = 8$

(5) $3n - 5 = 10$

(6) $4p - 3 = 33$

(7) $10 - 2q = 8$

(8) $15 - 4r = 1$

(9) $4s + 7 = 87$

(10) $5t - 6 = 49$

(11) $20 - 3w = 4$

(12) $\frac{x}{2} + 3 = 8$

(13) $9 - \frac{a}{4} = 7$

(14) $12 - \frac{y}{2} = 8$

(15) $\frac{21}{z} + 8 = 11$

Write an equation for each of the following and then solve it:

68

(1) n is a number. Double it and add 5. The result is 23. Find n.

(2) a is a number. Multiply the number by 5 and then subtract 8. If the answer is 22, find the number.

(3) Add three times the number b to 7 and the answer is 31. Find b.

(4) When four times a number is subtracted from 22, the result is 10. What is the number?

(5) x is a number. Treble it and add 17. The result is 32. Find the number.

(6) On subtracting half of a certain number from 11, the result is 6. Find the number.

(7)

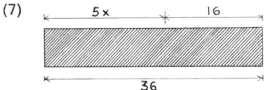

Find x

(8) On a journey into town a boy walks 2 kilometres and then travels 4x kilometres on a bus. If the total length of his journey is 10 kilometres, find x.

(9) Tom, Dick and Harry have each got n pence. Their friend Charles has 14 pence. The four boys have altogether 35 pence. How much money has Tom?

(10) Nicola is 5 years older than her sister Karen who is y years old. Together their ages total 27 years. How old is Nicola?

The Circle

Abe has another shape:

The circle has:
(1) A *centre* marked A.
(2) A boundary line or perimeter called the *circumference.*
(3) A *radius* which is the distance from the *centre* to the *circumference.*
(4) A *diameter* which is a straight line through the *centre* joining two points on the *circumference.*

Abe studies!

Abe's Circle Code

> If for any circle,
> C is the measure of the length of the Circumference,
> D is the measure of the length of the Diameter, and
> r is the measure of the length of the Radius,
> then, $D = 2 \times r$ or $D = 2r$

69 **Assignment 1:** Using a pencil and a pair of compasses draw, using different centres, circles having the following radii:

(1) 3 cm   (2) 5 cm   (3) 4 cm   (4) 2 cm   (5) 4·5 cm

70 **Assignment 2:** Draw, using the same centre, the set of circles with radii 3 cm, 5 cm, 4 cm and 2 cm.

TRY ABE'S ASSIGNMENT

Note: You require pencil, compasses, thread or string.

(1) Draw a circle of radius 5 cm.

(2) Draw a diameter in your circle.

(3) Measure the length of the Diameter (D cm).

(4) Using thread or string measure, as accurately as you can, the length of the Circumference (C cm).

(5) Find the value of $\dfrac{C}{D}$ correct to 2 decimal places.

(6) Repeat this assignment for other circles of radii 4 cm, 3 cm and 6 cm and for two circular lids or wheels of different sizes.

(7) Copy and complete the following table for different circles:

A TABLE FOR CIRCLES						
Circle	Length of Circumference	Length of Diameter	C	D	$\dfrac{C}{D}$	Value of C/D
Abe's	31·4 cm	10 cm	31·4	10	$\dfrac{31·4}{10}$	3·14
1						
2						
3						
1st lid						
2nd lid						

You should have found that in your last column of the table the answers are 3·14 approximately.

The value of $\dfrac{C}{D}$ for all circles is represented by the Greek symbol π read as pi.

π has an approximate value of 3·14 for all circles.

Abe says

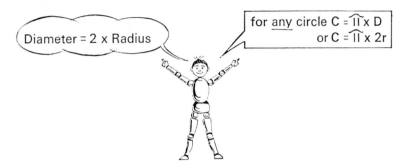

Abe finds the circumference of
a circle of diameter 23 cm.

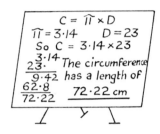

REMEMBER: π = 3·14 (approximately)

Find the length of the circumference for circles having:

72

(1) Radius = 5 cm   (2) Radius = 7·5 cm   (3) Radius = 17·5 cm

(4) Diameter = 30 cm   (5) Diameter = 45 cm   (6) Diameter = 55 cm

Abe's Mixtures

73

(1) A circle has a diameter of 15 cm. Find the length of its circumference.

(2) The radius of a bicycle wheel is 32·5 cm. Find the circumference of the wheel.

(3) A circular pond has a diameter of 35 metres.

     (a) What length of fencing is needed to enclose the pond?

     (b) What will the fencing cost at 22 p/m?

(4) A wheel has a circumference of 60 cm. How many turns will it make in travelling a distance of 54 metres?

(5) How many revolutions will a wheel of circumference 32 cm make when travelling 64 kilometres?

Squares and Square Roots

Square Numbers

74

(1) Make square dot patterns to represent:

    (a) 4   (b) 25   (c) 36   (d) 16   (e) 9   (f) 64

(2) By copying and completing the following table give the number of dots in each side of the square dot patterns you have drawn for (1).

Square Number	Side
4	
25	
36	
16	
9	
64	
100	
81	
49	

(3) Dot patterns are used to represent square numbers. How many dots are in the sides of the squares representing:

    (a) 49   (b) 64   (c) 100 (d) 144 (e) 81   (f) 121

(4) Find the value of the following products:

    (a) 11×11 (b) 9×9 (c) 4×4 (d) 13×13

    (e) 12×12 (f) $1 \cdot 1 \times 1 \cdot 1$ (g) $1 \cdot 3 \times 1 \cdot 3$ (h) $1 \cdot 2 \times 1 \cdot 2$

    (i) $0 \cdot 9 \times 0 \cdot 9$ (j) $2 \cdot 5 \times 2 \cdot 5$

Abe Says

The Square of 4 is written as 4^2 or $4 \times 4 = 16$
The Square of 9 is written as 9^2 or $9 \times 9 = 81$

The number of dots in the side of the Dot Pattern representing a Square Number gives the square Root of that number. Thus 9 is the square root of 81, written $9 = \sqrt{81}$.

(5) Find the values of:

(a) 15^2 (b) 17^2 (c) 18^2 (d) 9^2

(e) 25^2 (f) 23^2 (g) $1 \cdot 4^2$ (h) $1 \cdot 8^2$

(i) $2 \cdot 3^2$ (j) $3 \cdot 2^2$ (k) $\sqrt{15^2}$ (l) $\sqrt{17 \times 17}$

(m) $\sqrt{16}$ (n) $\sqrt{25}$ (o) $\sqrt{81}$ (p) $\sqrt{196}$

(q) $\sqrt{6 \cdot 25}$ (r) $\sqrt{1 \cdot 44}$ (s) $\sqrt{1 \cdot 21}$ (t) $\sqrt{1}$

Useful Tables

Table of Squares

Number (N)	Square (N^2)
1	$1^2 = 1$
2	$2^2 = 4$
3	$3^2 = 9$
4	$4^2 = 16$
5	$5^2 = 25$
6	36
7	49
8	64
9	81
10	100
11	121
12	144
13	169
14	196
15	225
16	256
20	400
25	625

Table of Square Roots

Number (N)	Square Root ($\sqrt{N}$)
1	1
4 (∴∵)	2
9 (∷)	3
16	4
25	5
36	6
49	7
64	8
81	9
100	10
121	11
144	12
169	13
196	14
225	15
256	16
400	20
625	25

Using the above tables:

(1) Write down the Square of:

(a) 2   (b) 4   (c) 3   (d) 7   (e) 9   (f) 14   (g) 13   (h) 16

(2) Write down the Square Root of:

(a) 4   (b) 16   (c) 9   (d) 25   (e) 36   (f) 49   (g) 64

(3) Find the answers to:

(a) $\sqrt{81}$ (b) $\sqrt{100}$ (c) $\sqrt{144}$ (d) $\sqrt{400}$ (e) $\sqrt{4 \cdot 00}$ (f) $\sqrt{0 \cdot 16}$

75

Area of Circle

Abe Looks at the Area of a Circle

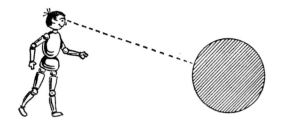

Do Abe's Assignment carefully.

(1) Draw and cut out a circle of radius 4 cm.

(2) Draw one diameter in your circle. Fold the circle along the diameter.

(3) Cut along the diameter with a pair of scissors.

(4) Fold each semi-circle in two and cut along the fold.

(5) Fold each of your four pieces exactly in two and cut along the fold.

(6) Repeat this operation for the eight pieces you now have.

(7) You should now have sixteen pieces each of exactly the same area.

(8)
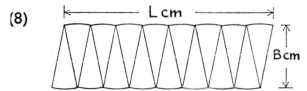

Fit your pieces together as in the diagram.

(9) Measure the length (L cm) of your figure and measure its breadth (B cm).

(10) Multiply L by B

(11) If $\pi = 3 \cdot 14$ and $R^2 = 16$ what is the value of $\pi \times R^2$?
Does your answer approximate to $L \times B$?

(12) Copy this statement.
The area of a circle is given by $A = \pi R^2$.

Area of a Circle

$$A = \pi R^2 \qquad \qquad A = \pi R^2$$

$$\pi = 3.14$$

Find the area of a circular arena with a diameter of 8 metres.

Says Abe,

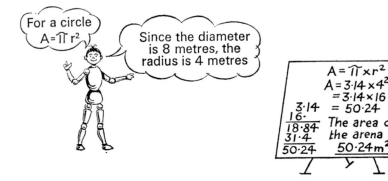

76

(1) Find the areas of the circles with:

(a) radius = 3 cm

(b) radius = 6 cm

(c) radius = 10 cm

(d) diameter = 16 cm

(e) diameter = 10 cm

(f) diameter = 18 cm

(g) radius = 12 cm

(h) radius = 16 cm

(i) radius = 15 cm

(j) radius = 20 cm

(2) What is the area of a circular flower bed of radius 7 metres?

(3) A circular plot of ground 32 metres in diameter has to be sown with grass seed which cost 40p/kg. What will be the cost of seed if one kilogramme is required for 4 square metres? (Give your answer correct to the nearest penny.)

(4) What is the cost of laying a circular tiled floor of radius 2 metres if the charge for labour and materials is £5·00/m²?

Operations on Sets—Union, Intersection

OPERATIONS ON SETS

∪, ∩

In Arithmetic you have performed the operations named Addition, Subtraction, Multiplication and Division on numbers. Now you are ready to perform the **operations named Union and Intersection on sets.**

UNION OF SETS

∪

In the Venn Diagram, A = {3, 6, 9}

B = {1, 3, 5, 7, 9}

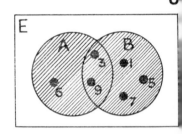

The shaded region contains all the members of A and B.

This set, {1, 3, 5, 6, 7, 9} is called the *Union* of A and B.

We write, {1, 3, 5, 6, 7, 9} = A ∪ B   or   A ∪ B = {1, 3, 5, 7, 9}

We say, Set A *union* set B is the set containing the members 1, 3, 5, 6, 7 and 9.

Note: The union of two sets is that set containing all the members of the two sets with no member repeated.

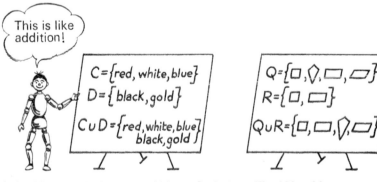

(1)   X = {1, 3, 5, 7} and Y = {2, 4, 6}. Find X ∪ Y.

(2)   C = {2, 4, 6, 8} and Y = {2, 4, 6}. Find C ∪ Y.

(3)   P = {5, 10, 15, 20} and Q = {9, 10, 11}. Find P ∪ Q.

(4)   V = {a, e, i, o, u} and W = {x, y, z}. Find V ∪ W.

(5)   B = {c, l, a, s} and S = {s, c, h, o, l}. Find B ∪ S.

(6)   P = {2, 3, 5, 7}, T = {2, 4, 6, 8} and O = {1, 3, 5, 7}.

   Find: (a) P ∪ T   (b) P ∪ O   (c) T ∪ O

(7) Using sets P, T and O in question (6):

    (a) Find: (i) $T \cup P$ (ii) $O \cup P$ (iii) $O \cup T$.

    (b) Study your answers to (6) and (7). Is the Commutative Law true for the union of sets?

(8) $X = \{2, 4, 6\}$ $Y = \{3, 6, 9\}$ and $Z = \{3, 6, 12\}$.

    (a) Find: (i) $X \cup Y$ (ii) $Y \cup Z$.

    (b) Find: (i) $(X \cup Y) \cup Z$ (ii) $X \cup (Y \cup Z)$.

    (c) $(X \cup Y) \cup Z = X \cup (Y \cup Z)$ implies a certain law is true for the union of sets. Which law is it?

INTERSECTION OF SETS   ∩

In the Venn Diagram, $A = \{3, 6, 9, 12\}$.

                      $B = \{2, 4, 6, 8, 10, 12\}$.

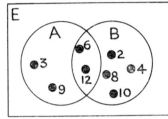

The shaded region contains all the members common to A and B.

This set, $\{6, 12\}$, is called the *Intersection* of A and B.

We write, $\{6, 12\} = A \cap B$ or $A \cap B = \{6, 12\}$.

We say, Set A, *intersection* set B is the set containing the members 6 and 12.

Note: The intersection of two sets is that set containing all the members common to the two sets.

$C = \{red, white, blue\}$
$D = \{black, gold\}$
$C \cap D = \{\}$ or $\emptyset$

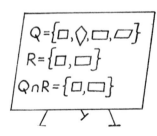

$Q = \{\square, \lozenge, \square, \square\}$
$R = \{\square, \square\}$
$Q \cap R = \{\square, \square\}$

(1) What is the intersection of sets E and F where $E = \{2, 4, 6, 8, 10\}$ and $F = \{4, 8, 12\}$?

(2) $B = \{John, Ian, Jack\}$ and $G = \{May, Jane, Liz\}$. Find $B \cap G$.

(3) $L = \{a, b, c, d, e\}$ and $M = \{c, a, b\}$. Find $L \cap M$.

(4) $P = \{3, 6, 9\}$ and $Q = \{1, 3, 5, 7, 9\}$. Find $P \cap Q$.

(5) $X = \{2, 3, 5, 7, 11\}$, $Y = \{1, 2, 4, 8\}$ and $Z = \{2, 4, 6, 8\}$.
Find: (a) $X \cap Y$ (b) $X \cap Z$ (c) $Y \cap Z$

(6) $S = \{\checkmark, \square, \triangle\}$ and $T = \{\square, \triangle, \checkmark\}$. Find $S \cap T$.

78

(7) A = {1, 2, 4, 7, 11 } B = {1, 4, 9, 16 } and C = {1, 2, 4, 8, 16 }.
Find: (a) A ∩ B   (b) B ∩ A   (c) A ∩ C
       (d) C ∩ A   (e) B ∩ C   (f) C ∩ B
       (g) (A ∩ B) ∩ C   (h) A ∩ (B ∩ C)

(8) Refer to your answers for question (7):
     (a) Is the Commutative Law true for the intersection of sets?
     (b) (A ∩ B) ∩ C = A ∩ (B ∩ C) implies a certain law is true for the intersection of sets. Which law is it?

(9) P is the set of prime numbers less than 10. O is the set of odd numbers less than 10.
     (a) Draw a Venn Diagram to illustrate the sets O and P.
     (b) List the set O ∪ P.
     (c) Shade the set O ∩ P.

A TEST — 'SETS   {e, s, t }

79

(1) From the answer set, { ∅, ∩, ∈, ∉, ⊂, E, ∪ }; write the appropriate symbol to represent:
     (a) is a member of   (b) is a subset of   (c) intersection
     (d) is not a member of   (e) the universal set   (f) union
     (g) the empty set

(2)

From the Venn Diagram:
     (a) List set A   (b) List set B
     (c) List set A ∪ B   (d) List set A ∩ B
     (e) List an appropriate universal set.
     (f) Is 9 ∈ A?   (g) Is 9 ∈ B?
     (h) Is 3 ∉ B true?
     (i) List the set of multiples of 5 which are members of set A.
     (j) Which of the following statements are true?
         (i) A ⊂ E   (ii) A ⊂ B
         (iii) B ⊂ A   (iv) B ⊂ E.
     (k) Which set is the largest subset of both sets A and B?

(3) (a) Draw a Venn Diagram to represent the sets:
         E = {1, 2, 3, 4, 5, 6, 7, 8, 9, 10 }, P = {1, 3, 5, 7, 9 } and Q = {2, 4, 6, 8 }
     (b) Shade the regions representing P ∪ Q.
     (c) State set P ∩ Q.

Progress Checks 7-9

Formulae: Circumference of circle $= 2\pi R$ $\pi = 3\cdot14$
Area of Circle $= \pi R^2$
Volume of Cuboid $=$ LBH

PROGRESS CHECK 7

(1) For a transaction CP = £8·35. SP = £10·12. Find the profit if there are no overheads.

(2) The rate of exchange of Spanish currency is 170 pesetas to the £. Convert £18·50 into pesetas.

(3) During a year the total sales of a newsagent amounted to £18 035. If his purchases amounted to £13 742 and his overheads were £2 856, find his total profit.

(4) Using the scale 1 cm represents 20 m, find the distances represented by lines with the following measurements:

  (a) 3 cm   (b) 5 cm   (c) 10·5 cm

(5) Find the value of 4^3. Write your answer as a power of 2.

(6) A = {1, 3, 5, 7 }   B = {2, 6 }   Find A $\cup$ B

(7) Solve the equation: $4x + 7 = 39$.

(8) A running track is in the shape of a circle 100 metres in diameter. What is the length of one lap of the track?

(9) Find the area of a circle with a radius of 9 metres.

(10) A water tank is in the shape of a cuboid 6 m long, 4 m broad and 2·5 m high. How many cubic metres of water will it hold?

PROGRESS CHECK 8

(1) CP = £91·12 and SP = £102·20. Find the profit if the overheads amounted to £5.

(2) A school buys 4 cartons of crisps, each containing 50 packets, for £4·60 The crisps are sold at 3p per packet. Find the total profit if overheads amount to £0·32.

(3) The scale factor on a plan is 1:50. Find the length of line on the plan required to prepresent:

  (a) 25 cm   (b) 175 cm   (c) 3·5 m.

(4) C = {2, 4, 6, 8, 10 }   D = {1, 2, 4, 8 }   Find C $\cap$ D.

(5) The distance from the Earth to the Sun is $1\cdot49 \times 10^8$ km. How far is half of this distance?

(6) Solve for x: $19 - 3x = 1$.

(7) A man earns £1 500 in a year. Find, to the nearest new penny, his average wage in a week.

(8) n is a number. Treble it and subtract 6. The result is 15. Form an equation and find the number.

(9) At a Rally-Cross Meeting there is a race over 4 laps of a circular track 100 metres in diameter. Find the length of the race in kilometres.

(10) The tank which feeds the pump at a petrol station is cuboidal in shape. The measurements of the tank are 400 cm by 300 cm by 150 cm. How many litres of petrol will the tank hold when full? (1 litre $= 1\ 000$ cm^3)

PROGRESS CHECK 9

(1) The exchange rate for the U.S.A. dollar is $2·40/£1. Find the value in British money of a stereo disc which sells in New York at $5·52.

(2) The total sales of a Baker for the year amount to £12 684. If his purchases total £5 972 and his overheads are £4 285, find his total profit.

(3) Two plans are made of the same piece of ground. Plan A uses the scale 1 cm represents 2 m. Plan B uses the scale 1 cm represents 4 m. What length of line on each drawing represents 20 metres?

(4) X = {1, 2, 3, 4, 5, 6, 7, 8 }   Y = {4, 9, 10 }
Find   (a) X $\cup$ Y   (b) X $\cap$ Y

(5) Draw a Venn Diagram to represent the sets in question (4).

(6) A chemist sells a perfume in two sizes of bottles, 7 cm^3 and 20 cm^3. A small bottle of perfume is sold at £1·05 and a large bottle at £2·40. Find the selling price of 1 cm^3 of perfume from each size of bottle.

(7) Find in metric tonnes, the weight of an ingot of steel 4·5 m long, 2 m broad and 1 m high. (1 m^3 of steel weighs 8 metric tonnes).

(8) Find the perimeter of the playing field shown in the diagram:

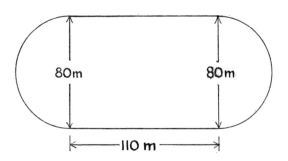